Start Young!

Early Childhood Science Activities

Start Young!

Early Childhood Science Activities

Shannan McNair, Editor

NATIONAL SCIENCE TEACHERS ASSOCIATION

Arlington, Virginia

Claire Reinburg, Director
Judy Cusick, Senior Editor
Andrew Cocke, Associate Editor
Betty Smith, Associate Editor
Robin Allan, Book Acquisitions Coordinator

Cover, Inside Design, and Illustrations by Linda Olliver

Printing and Production Catherine Lorrain-Hale, Director
 Nguyet Tran, Assistant Production Manager
 Jack Parker, Electronic Prepress Technician
 Linda Olliver, Cover and Book Design

National Science Teachers Association
Gerald F. Wheeler, Executive Director
David Beacom, Publisher

Library of Congress Cataloging-in-Publication Data

Start young! : early childhood science activities / Shannan McNair, editor.
    p. cm.
 Includes bibliographical references.
 ISBN-13: 978-0-87355-268-4
 ISBN-10: 0-87355-268-7
 1. Science—Study and teaching (Early childhood)—Activity programs—United States. I. McNair, Shannan.
 Q183.3.A1S68 2005
 372.35'0440973—dc22
                        2005029522

 Featuring sciLINKS® —a new way of connecting text and the internet. Up-to-the-minute online content, classroom ideas, and other materials are just a click away.

Contents

Introduction vii
Quick Reference Chart xii

Early Learning and Science

Start Young! 3
Kids Questioning Kids: "Experts Sharing" 7
What the Real Experts Say 15
How Big Is Big? How Small Is Small? 21

Child-Centered Curricula

The Bird 29
Gravitating Toward Reggio 33
Spideriffic Learning Tools 39
It's a Frog's Life 45
Science Centers for All 53
Project Reptile! 57
A Science Night of Fun 65

Integrating Curricula

First Flight 73
Tracking Through the Tulips 79
The Science and Mathematics of Building Structures 85
Discovery Central 93
Ladybugs Across the Curriculum 97
Miniature Sleds, Go, Go, Go! 105
Journey Into the Five Senses 113

Assessing Understanding

Drawing on Student Understanding 121
The Tree of Life 129
Students' Ideas About Plants 135
Let's Try Action Research! 145
Playful Activities for Young Children 151

INDEX 159

Introduction

Children learn science from infancy, observing and responding to the phenomena in their daily experience. They learn about their immediate environment through their senses of sight, sound, touch, smell, and taste. When babies become mobile, they explore the world around them more rapidly. Then they start using trial and error, repetition, imitation, and classification. Children who are exposed from babyhood to a wealth of experiences through active exploration are laying a foundation for the development of science concepts later. They use science process skills as they move from observation and exploration during the toddler years to data collection, classification, representation, communicating theories, and interpretation in the preschool and primary years.

Caregivers for and teachers of young children can easily underestimate the capability young children have for science learning and miss spontaneous opportunities for supporting science learning. But they should learn to for purposeful exploration and experimentation. Children love science experiences and are fascinated by even the smallest aspect of the world around them. Seeing young children as curious, competent, and interested science learners is a good beginning. Using this book as a resource is a next step.

The National Science Education Teaching Standards (NSES) (NRC 1996) direct teachers toward high-quality science teaching with clear criteria describing what teachers can do to support science learners at all age levels. Teaching Standard A criteria tell teachers "to select science content and adapt and design curricula to meet the interests, knowledge, understanding, abilities, and experiences of students." The articles in this book will help teachers do just that. They provide teachers with activities for young children that connect to the National Science Education Standards and will result in better science teaching and children more interested in learning.

Early Learning and Science

Current findings from brain research and a resurgence in interest in the very young child as a learner makes this an exciting time for early childhood educators, but a time not without challenges. The emphasis on literacy as an isolated curriculum area has resulted in either the virtual exclusion of science experiences for young children or a limited, surface treatment of science instruction in preschool and primary settings. This section highlights articles from authors who emphasize the need to start young and provide opportunities for science learning that use the capabilities young children bring to science investigation.

In "Start Young!" Penni Rubin relates how interviews with scientists nationwide revealed a common experience—exposure to meaningful science experiences at an early age. She suggests this knowledge can be applied in classrooms by providing interesting adult role models and classroom experiences that connect science concepts to real world careers, professionals, and daily experience. She goes on to provide useful suggestions for setting up age-appropriate career learning centers to promote interest and learning in chemistry, botany, zoology, oceanography, Earth science, and paleontology.

Science learning is enhanced through conversations among children, the focus in Marletta Iwasyk's "Kids Questioning Kids: Experts Sharing." She describes ways in which documenting the conversations of children reveals their understanding and interest and provides insights into effective questioning strategies.

In "What the Real Experts Say," a first-grade teacher describes her journey of putting theory learned in a professional development seminar into practice in her classroom. Teaching first graders the scientific process seemed impossible to Carol Avila until she tried this application of the National Science Education Standards. Listening to the responses of her students during a science demonstration, asking questions related to the students' comments, and supporting their investigation convinced her that her first-grade students were the real experts.

Young children ask important questions about the world around them. "How Big Is Big: How Small Is Small" connects National Science Education Standards to young children's questions about relative size. The vivid descriptions of second-grade students studying drawings and text, collecting data on their own observations, and demonstrating their knowledge to other students invite instant application.

Active Science Learning

The articles in this section describe science learning that is student-centered: Teachers plan learning experiences with children based upon the questions the children generate, the ideas and interest they evidence, and the knowledge and skills they bring to the classroom. Taking advantage of teachable moments takes a high level of skill and awareness, and facilitating the construction of scientific concepts is challenging. Teachers must provide thought-provoking materials and meaningful activities and do so for learners who come from a variety of cultural and ethnic backgrounds and have diverse abilities and skills.

In "The Bird," one teacher tells how she used students' finding a bird dead on the school playground to promote science learning in her classroom. "Gravitating Toward Reggio" by Josephine Shireen DeSouza and Jill Jereb gives readers insight into the Reggio

Emilia schools whose innovative, high-quality practices are drawing international attention. Schools for young children in Reggio Emilia, Italy, base their teaching practice on the premise that young children are capable of investigating important questions in depth and reflecting on their learning experiences. Teachers demonstrate respect for children as they listen carefully to children's explanations and theories, observe their learning processes, and plan experiences to expand upon their interests. These schools inspired the authors to apply Reggio Emilia principles to an in-depth investigation of forces and motion in their primary classroom.

In "Spideriffic Learning Tools," Kevin Mitchell and Keith Diem give readers a look at the Spideriffic curriculum they developed to teach broad science concepts by using real-world creatures and settings. Students are often both fearful and fascinated by spiders and hold many misconceptions about these intriguing arthropods. This article is filled with facts about spiders and practical classroom learning experiences.

In "It's a Frog's Life," Audrey Coffey and Donna Sterling offer an account of inquiry conducted by preschool learners after Coffey and Sterling took advantage of a teachable moment when frogs laid eggs in the preschool pool. Deborah Diffily, in "Project Reptile," details the advantages for learners when experiences are child-centered and integrate content areas. She describes an in-depth project of building a reptile exhibit in her kindergarten.

Every teacher works to provide learning experiences appealing and appropriate to a diverse group of students. Leslie Irwin, Christine Nucci, and Carol Beckett, in "Science Centers for All," emphasize the importance of equity in science learning and suggest strategies for effectively supporting diverse learners. They describe using science centers to provide challenging, high-interest, open-ended science investigations and give suggestions for promoting collaboration, allocating space, and selecting materials.

"A Science Night of Fun" from Katie Rommel-Esham and Andrea Castellitto involves the community—teachers, students, families, and members of the community experts in the field—in science learning.

Integrating Curricula

The younger the child, the more integrated his or her learning experiences can be. Integrating a high-interest, concept-laden subject area such as science into language, literacy, and mathematics learning increases student engagement and allows for more natural application of knowledge and skills to real-life tasks. Process skills are similar across areas of the curriculum, so practice with the skills of observation, exploration, inquiry, data collection, reflection, and interpretation can take place throughout the school day and across content areas.

Phyllis Whitin details bird-watching in "First Flight" as a yearlong kindergarten classroom investigation aimed at learning about the nature of science and the real-life tasks of scientists. "Tracking Through the Tulips" by Dorothy Davis tells about an online learning experience supported by funds from a Toyota Tapestry Grant —coupled with planting experiences—both real and virtual—that connect to the Standards.

Ingrid Chalufour, Cindy Hoisington, Robin Moriarty, Jeff Winokur, and Karen Worth describe how preschool children conduct inquiry while exploring relationships and discovering properties of materials in "The Science and Mathematics of Building Structures." They emphasize how experiences that normally take place in classrooms offer the richest science inquiry.

Inquiry is key in "Discovery Central" as Jaimee Wood shows how she supported critical thinking in a kindergarten classroom using a plant unit with integrated experiences such as sorting, painting, listening, and writing. Similarly, in "Ladybugs Across the Curriculum," Christina Dias Ward and Michael Dias describe a crosscurricular experience with ladybugs and detail how they addressed multiple intelligences through the project.

Gina Sarow used a learning model, Design Technology: Children's Engineering, to supplement the regular curriculum each month with design technology learning. "Miniature Sleds, Go, Go, Go!" describes the projects students constructed while using real tools, drawing their plans or blueprints, and building their models.

In "Journey Into the Five Senses," Susan McWilliams, while a doctoral student researching inquiry teaching and learning, witnessed a primary teacher of K–2 students take them on a journey through the five senses. She describes how hands-on experiences, field trips, guest experts, and books promoted the development of conceptual understanding.

Assessing Understanding

The NSES emphasize learning and assessment as a simultaneous process in that teachers plan for assessment at the same time they plan the learning experiences. Diverse strategies for authentic classroom assessment as-

sure that all learners have opportunities to show in a variety of ways what they know and can do. Student demonstrations, representations, presentations, documentation, and samples of work are examples of multiple methods of classroom assessment that accommodate diverse learning styles. Ongoing, formative assessment provides a window to student learning that informs teacher planning and the implementation of meaningful and relevant science experiences for the children.

Assessment that helps teachers identify conceptual understanding before and after a set of lessons, or a unit, and helps them determine where misunderstanding or misconceptions exist in individual children leads to more effective instruction for transfer and learning that lasts. Assessment embedded in the learning experience, in which students are assessed while they are learning, makes the most of instructional time. Assessment that is transparent to students supports their learning by helping them reflect on their own learning styles, accomplishments, and goals. Assessment of problem solving and critical thinking helps teachers foster higher-level thinking.

"Drawing on Student Understanding," authors—Mary Stein, Shannan McNair, and Jan Butcher—describe using drawing as a tool to help students develop and document more complex understanding. They share reasons for using art as a tool for deepening scientific concept knowledge and strategies for achieving success.

In "The Tree of Life," Donna M. Plummer, Jeannie MacShara, and Skila King Brown offer time-saving suggestions for integrating academic areas through the use of children's literature, while at the same time documenting student learning in science and literacy. For example, students demonstrated their knowledge of characteristics of organisms and the use of descriptive vocabulary through artistic representation and writing.

"Students' Ideas About Plants" describes a study invited by *Science and Children* that investigated students' ideas about plants and plant growth. Charles R. Barman, Mary Stein, Natalie S. Barman, and I related study results to the Standards. A table outlining student misconceptions reveals how to teach to address the misconceptions. "Let's Try Action Research" documents another study invited by *Science and Children*. It inspired authors Ginger Stovall and Catherine R. Nesbit to replicate the Assessing Students' Ideas About Animals study (Barman et al. 1999) that determined the misconceptions students had about what makes an animal an animal and investigating whether or not a constructivist approach alters misconceptions. These two articles provide examples of assessment that contributes feedback to science educators about science learning.

"Playful Activities for Young Children" by Smita Guha and Rodney Doran ends this volume with a description of assessment tasks for younger students that demand little reading and writing—observing their science understanding through engaging activities. This approach can be applied to very young children in settings from home, to childcare and preschool.

In the Classroom

Teachers can support students through early exposure to science learning to develop a strong base for understanding science concepts, practice science process skills, and learn to explore questions about their everyday worlds using the inquiry process. Early science instruction can promote educational equity by introducing young children to the language of science, tools for science exploration, and processes for conducting inquiry.

Young children bring to the classroom natural curiosity about scientific phenomena that relates to their daily life and engage in constructive play around important science concepts. Babies explore the characteristics of objects with all of their senses and begin the process of organizing information into categories before they can speak. Toddlers are keen observers and imitators of what they see. Preschool children want to know the why and how of light switches, tadpoles, and thunderstorms. Teachers can build on this intense interest in science concepts in the early years to promote confidence and competence later in school. It is never too early to learn science.

Shannan McNair
Associate Professor
Oakland University, School of Education
Human Development and Child Studies
Rochester, Michigan

References

Barman, C. R., N. S. Barman, K. Berglund, and M. J. Goldston. 1999. Assessing students' ideas about animals. *Science and Children* 37 (1): 44–49.

National Research Council. 1996. *National Science Education Standards*. Washington, DC: National Academy Press.

Quick-Reference Chart of Articles

Article	Standards*	Page
Early Learning and Science		
Start Young!		3
Kids Questioning Kids: Experts Sharing		7
What the Real Experts Say		15
How Big Is Big?		21
Child-Centered Curricula		
The Bird		29
Gravitating Toward Reggio	Content Standards A and B	33
Spideriffic Learning Tools	Content Standards A, C, and E	39
It's a Frog's Life	Content Standards A and C	45
Science Centers for All		53
Project Reptile	Teaching Standards A, B, C, D, and E Content Standards A, C, E, and G	57
A Science Night of Fun	Teaching Standards A, B, D, and F Professional Development Standards A, B, and C Science Education Program Standards B, C, D, E, and F	65

(continued next page)

National Science Teachers Association

(continued from previous page)

Article	Standards*	Page
Integrating Curricula		
First Flight		73
Tracking Through the Tulips	Content Standards A, C, and D	79
The Science and Mathematics of Building Structures	Content Standard A and B	85
Discovery Central	Content Standard C	93
Ladybugs Across the Curriculum	Content Standards A and C	97
Miniature Sleds, Go, Go, Go!	Teaching Standards A, B, C, and D Content Standards A, B, and E	105
Journey Into the Five Senses	Content Standards A, C, and F	113
Assessing Understanding		
Drawing on Student Understanding		121
The Tree of Life	Content Standards A, C, and F	129
Students' Ideas About Plants	Content Standard C Content Standard C for grades 5–8	135
Let's Try Action Research	Content Standards A and C	145
Playful Activities for Young Children	Content Standards A and B	151

*All Standards refer to the National Science Education Standards for grades K–4 unless otherwise noted. (National Research Council. 1996. *National Science Education Standards.* Washington, DC: National Academy Press.)

Early Learning and Science

Start Young!

We need to give children a helping hand when they are most open-minded and curious.

Penni Rubin

While creating a children's science activity book for the U.S. Geological Survey (Rubin and Robbins 1992), I interviewed many scientists around the country. One question I asked of all these men and women was "When did your interest in your area of expertise begin?" This question arose because of my sister's long-standing interest in geology: As a child, she had played in the creek across the street from our house. As an adult, concepts taught in a college geology course resonated because of her childhood experiences watching the neighborhood creek change over the years.

I heard similar stories among the scientists I interviewed. For example, an oceanographer told me that it was during a vacation by the Atlantic Ocean at age seven when he first "fell in love with the ocean." Jack Horner, one of the top U.S. paleontologists, found his first dinosaur bone at age seven. I also heard from a volcanologist who knew she wanted to study volcanoes after seeing them on a trip out West with her parents when she was seven; an astronomer who remembered receiving a telescope as a child; and another astronomer who remembered using a telescope as a young child to investigate why the "Blue Moon" was not really blue. In a PBS interview, I heard Jane Goodall claiming that her favorite things as a child were the book *Dr. Doolittle* and a stuffed chimpanzee toy.

Every computer scientist, dentist, and engineer I talked with reported that, as children, they enjoyed taking things apart and building their own creations with erector sets. My sister who is a computer scientist liked to unscrew doorknobs and drawer handles with a plastic screwdriver, all at the young age of four. By age seven, she pleaded with our mother to take the car apart when our father was away at a conference. She promised to put it back together again by the time he returned.

Magic "Seven"

Through these anecdotal interactions with the scientific community and my family, I began to notice that most interests leading to a career seem to start in early childhood.

Throughout my interviews, I heard either, "at age seven I became interested in" or "I knew I wanted to do this since I was a child."

A person, place, or thing is what usually sparks those first memorable childhood impressions. Of course, we often do not study our newfound interests from the time of our personal enlightenment to adulthood, but early childhood interests are strong and they can have a powerful hold on us. Children usually show interest in many areas; but, I've observed one interest generally resurfaces as they get older. Often, it seems this interest—usually one from childhood—is the one that leads to a profession.

If children's interest in the natural world around them is heightened at a young age, why are most science education programs geared to middle and high school students? None of the numerous scientists I talked with mentioned finding their professional interests as teens or adults. They merely rediscovered their childhood interests at these ages.

In the Classroom

I strongly believe that the focus of science and mathematics exploration and activities should begin in preschool and kindergarten, before children develop negative connotations or become disengaged from the subjects. More important, early elementary school teachers and parents should exhibit a love and appreciation for science.

Some ideas for cultivating an early interest in science include the following:

- Set up career-oriented learning centers in the classroom for students. Supply these centers with "STUFF"—Stimulating Tools Useful for Fun and Fundamentals. (See the box on p. 5 for ideas.)

I began to notice that most interests leading to a career seem to start in early childhoood.

- Invite naturalists or scientists to the classroom. Have them bring the tools they use so they can demonstrate how they do their work and students can imagine how they do their jobs.

- Encourage children to have a hobby, such as collecting leaves, rocks, or shells. Visit the library to research their collections. These experiences can lead to discoveries about other fascinating subjects on the same shelf. Provide a show-and-tell showcase for children to share their collections and perhaps spark another student's imagination.

If we want to encourage children to enter into scientific fields in the future, we need to give them a helping hand while they are most open-minded and curious. Answer children's questions with questions, such as "What do you think?" or "What do you know," to find out what they already know about a topic. Then you can guide them with some clues on how to find the answers, which makes children responsible for their own learning. It's okay not to hold all the

Early Childhood Career Learning Centers

To create a career-oriented learning center in the classroom, set up three long folding tables in a "T" or "U" shape and drape colorful plastic cloths over them.

Children tend to gravitate toward tools, so have a variety on hand, such as magnifying glasses, magnets, clipboards, graph paper, rulers, eyedroppers, funnels, and scoops. Some children also enjoy dressing up, so have swim flippers, hard hats, or a life jacket and other items for those more active students. (I once contacted a local laundry service that donated a bunch of small, white short-sleeved shirts to use as lab coats.)

The following are some career centers I've set up in classrooms:

- **Kitchen Chemistry:** Use clear containers with numbers and measuring tools to learn the properties of water. Work with gelatin, Popsicles, and pudding. Mix colors with eyedroppers and food dye or finger paint. Experiment with cornstarch and water on a cookie tray to see how a substance can be both a liquid and a solid.
- **Nutrition/Botany:** Create a storefront with plastic fruits and vegetables, empty food boxes, and a play cash register with play money. Make lists of questions about the foods such as "How does your family use plants? What plant parts do you eat?" Display pictures and posters of the good foods we eat. Collect leaves to press in a phone book.
- **Zoology:** Make a miniature zoo with stuffed animals, or hide a bunch of rubber snakes under a table with branches and a meterstick to measure and observe. Paint cardboard boxes as different habitat puppet stages and make animal puppets that would live in each habitat, using the box as a stage for a show.
- **Oceanography:** Sort seashells by bivalves and univalves with tweezers and tongs. Do crayon rubbings using textures that look like coral.
- **Earth Science:** Wet porous and nonporous rocks with water and an eyedropper. Make a sifter to separate and clean water. Create a mine shaft under a table with flashlights, pretend coal, fake gold, and a book about rocks and minerals.
- **Paleontology:** Create dig sites in clear plastic storage bins with mulch, sawdust, or gravel. Provide a bird or dinosaur skeleton picture for reference. Provide tweezers, tongs, and paintbrushes for students to sift through the debris and mark findings on grids.

While children explore these career-oriented learning centers, teachers can facilitate their learning. I use the following process:

Describe what the child is doing;

Compare something and suggest a tool;

Ask a leading question; and

Use narrative descriptive praise, such as, "When you did *this,* I noticed *that!*"

For example, at the oceanology center, the model might work something like this:

1. I saw you looking at the stingray and the sharks under the table;
2. Do you think they are also related to the whales and dolphins?;
3. I wonder if there's a chart in this book that will tell you if they are related. Shall we check it out?; and
4. I saw you reading that book. Was there something interesting that you could teach me about?

In the paleontology center, a typical exchange might be:

1. I noticed you took the chicken bones out of the sandbox before you recorded them on the chart;
2. I see there are letters and numbers on the sides of the bin;
3. I wonder if you could write down where each bone was found, just like real paleontologists do; and
4. I saw you figured out how to chart where all the bones were found! You sure stuck to that job. You should be very proud of yourself.

answers—what's important is taking the journey *with* children. Who knows? There may be a future scientist or two sitting in your classroom.

Penni Rubin runs workshops for preK–primary educators on interdisciplinary science. She can be reached at www.pennirubin.com.

Resources

Hann, J. 1991. *How science works*. New York: Reader's Digest Adults.

Holt, B. G. 1989. *Science with young children*. Washington, DC: National Association for the Education of Young Children.

Nichols, W., and K. Nichols. 1990. *Wonderscience: A developmentally appropriate guide to hands-on science for young children*. New Mexico: Learning Expo.

Paulu, N. 1992. *Helping your child learn science*. Washington, DC: U.S. Department of Education.

Redleaf, R. 1983. *Open the door let's explore*. St. Paul, MN: Toys and Things.

Rubin, P., and E. Robbins. 1992. *What's under your feet?* Reston, VA: U.S. Geological Survey.

Kids Questioning Kids: "Experts" Sharing

Children grow in their own skills as they teach others.

Marletta Iwasyk

As a kindergarten/first-grade teacher in an alternative school, I have much latitude in curriculum development and instructional methods. Questioning and dialog are an integral part of my teaching. The National Science Education Standards (NSES) say, "Inquiry into authentic questions generated from student experiences is the central strategy for teaching science" (NRC 1996, p. 31). I believe that children are capable of being teachers and while engaged in the teaching process, they reinforce and solidify their own learning.

To examine how this happens in my classroom, I conducted a case study to show children using questioning and communication skills during conversations about science (van Zee et al. 1997). The case study involved analysis of transcripts of students discussing the subject of shadows in which two students became the teachers or leaders and the rest asked questions for clarification or gave input of their own.

To document the discussions, I used a tape recorder with a microphone placed on a desk near the seated children. I also placed a video camera high in an unobtrusive corner. The camera was trained on the seats in the middle of the circle where I placed the leaders of the discussion. If other students had something to contribute, I asked them to step to the middle of the circle where I knew they would be visible to the camera. The object of this case study was to record the children's talk about shadows to see if there was any carryover from the teacher-directed questioning and discussion activities. The study focused on not only the facts being presented but also how the discussions took place.

Emphasis on Communication

From the first day of school, I model questioning and communication skills that I hope the children will emulate as the year progresses. Groups and pairs of children are allowed to converse a great deal during the day and so are comfortable speaking with one another.

The emphasis one year for the entire school was using kind and respectful words. I also stressed the role of a respectful listener, which provides an environment in which children feel they are safe to risk speaking and sharing their ideas. As a class, we practiced listening and speaking skills in many subject areas.

During show-and-tell time each week, the class president facilitated the sharing period, and the person called upon to share, in turn, asked for questions and comments from the rest of the class. As children responded to one another, I helped them analyze and decide whether they were making a direct comment about what they heard. In the beginning, many children added to the sharing—"I have a dog too"—rather than commenting on what was said. Also, their questions were usually too specific when asking for more information about what was shared—"Is your dog's name Rover or Fido?" We talked about a better way to ask the question—"What is your dog's name?"

Another opportunity for modeling questions came when the class president was interviewed for stories that were written by each individual for the "president's book." Again, early in the school year, the questions tended to be very specific and limited—"Do you like spaghetti? Do you like apples?" I encouraged the children to think in terms of general questions instead—"What is your favorite food or fruit? What do you like to do on the weekends?" This clarification helps children differentiate between types of responses and also determine appropriate times to make them. These skills carry over into other areas of study.

Emphasis on Science

Science is wonder—that feeling of awe and excitement you have when you see a golden harvest moon, experience the power of the wind, see a rainbow, watch a salmon hatching, or experience the miracles of nature that take place around you. My school, which has an environmental and art focus, greatly values this view of science and nurtures it in every child's heart and mind. It is then a natural step to go from this wonderland of experience and appreciation of nature to the world of discovery and the desire to find out the why and how.

And so, science is wondering as well, wondering about our physical and biological world—and young children wonder most of all. They have a natural, eager intellectual curiosity about the world around them and want to find out all they can, as evidenced by the many questions they ask. The dilemma for a teacher of young children is how to keep this natural curiosity alive within the confines of the classroom. Time, lack of materials or space, or other obstacles—such as a feeling of inadequacy in science knowledge—may limit the amount of experience the teacher provides in the area of science.

One successful activity I have used to keep this connection to the world outside the classroom is the study of light and shadows, using, of course, the most visible object in the children's sphere of reference—the Sun. Learning about objects in the sky, including observing the Sun and its movement, is one of the Benchmarks for Science Literacy for kindergarten through grade two (AAAS 1993). Much of my knowledge about the Sun was gained in a physics program for teachers at the University of Washington (McDermott 1995).

Activity Suggestions for Sun Plots and Shadows

- Take a walk on the playground and observe shadows of poles, trees, and walls.

- Take a walk with your shadow and observe how it follows wherever you go and does whatever you do.

- Have your class stand in a circle and discuss shadows they see—some are in front; some are behind. Discuss orientation if children want to make a claim about the shadow position. (If students say, "The shadows are in front of us," ask, "Are all the shadows in front?" If the children say no, then ask, "How can we make that happen?")

  Ask questions that help children see that everyone needs to be facing the same direction to see their shadow in front, behind, and so on. This can be facilitated by the use of a "shadow line" (discussed below) that is close to where your class lines up everyday. I have my class line up on the shadow line after every recess whether it is sunny or not. If it is sunny, then we can quickly make some observations, think about some questions, and have a short discussion before coming in—very efficient and easy to do. (At this time, I do not say whether a conclusion is right or wrong, I ask them to think about it.)

- Line up on a North-South line (if possible) on the playground. This orientation helps children see the shortest shadow pointing North at local noon. Give directions to your class, such as the following: "Stand so that your shadow is in front of you (or behind, beside on the left, right). Which way is your shadow pointing? Toward the building or away from it? Is it long or short? Longer or shorter than this morning's? Last

week's?" There are many questions you can ask to promote thinking and stimulate observations.

- Make a sun plot/shadow board (see illustration) for children to study shadows independently at home. To make the sun plot/shadow board, use heavy cardboard and stick a small nail (or other similar object) into the center. A sun plot/shadow board is placed in the same spot throughout the day. Children mark the end of the shadow (noting the time and date) using a piece of heavy cardboard with a sheet of white paper. Students can then observe the pattern the dots make, if connected.

- Train two children to use a sun plot/shadow board. Discuss the use of a gnomon, which is a straight object (peg, stick, rod) used to cast a shadow, and how to record data (length, time of day). Take as many readings as possible each day. The first team then trains the next team (a classroom job). If inside, shine a flashlight or bulb onto the sun plot board to make "artificial" shadows (Peg-Boards work well).

- On equinoxes and solstices, record the end of the shadow throughout the day on the playground with chalk and then use paint to make it permanent for future reference. A tall pole on a sturdy base works well as the gnomon for this—mark where the base goes.

- Transfer information from daily records to overlays for use on an overhead to compare fall, winter, and spring shadows (length, shape of line connecting dots, Sun's position). Overlays are good for end-of-year discussions.

- Enrich the activity with shadow puppets, poems, journal writing, and literature.

Sun Plot/Shadow Board
heavy cardboard with the sheet of paper

9:00 am 10:00 am 11:00 am 12:00 noon 1:00 pm 2:00 pm 3:00 pm

small peg (gnomon)

EQUINOX PATTERN

Figure 1. A KWHL Chart.

K	W	H	L
What do I **K**now about _____? (Prior knowledge, or preconceptions. All ideas are listed.)	What do I **W**ant to know about _____? (Questions that students have.)	**H**ow can I find out about _____? (Books, Internet, asking others.)	What did I **L**earn about _____? (Facts learned may be different from those listed on K.)

Shadow Discovery

On the very first sunny day of school in the fall, we begin our study of shadows. This is a natural and easy way not only to nurture curiosity and wondering, but also to help the children develop the skills and attitudes that will make them successful lifelong scientists, whether or not they go on to choose a career in a scientific field.

The box "Activity for Sun Plots and Shadows" lists some suggestions for shadow activities. These shadow activities entail making and comparing many observations and recordings throughout the year. Many questions arise, such as "Why does my shadow change shape, length, and direction?"

In the beginning, I do not answer any of the questions. Instead, I ask the children to think about the questions and discover how they can find the answers for themselves. If they make early conclusions about what they observe, I do not acknowledge any answer as right or wrong. It isn't until after the winter solstice, when the shadows are becoming short again, that we have an in-depth discussion of what we have learned about the Sun and shadows, with the children facilitating as

much as possible. To make this happen, much groundwork has been laid during the year.

Discussion of Shadows

Teaching Standard B states, "Teachers of science guide and facilitate learning. In doing this, teachers orchestrate discourse among students about scientific ideas" (NRC 1996, p. 32). See "Student Conversations" for an example of dialog that took place during a discussion of shadows, which typically lasts anywhere from 15 to 30 minutes, depending on interest and focus.

At the beginning of our discussion, the children posed questions they had thought about in connection with shadows, and these were listed on a KWHL chart—"Where do shadows come from? Can they see?"—see Figure 1.

In the course of the discussion, two male students who had a lot to share emerged as the facilitators for the discussions, calling on others for questions or comments. In giving the boys this role, I turned a possible negative—two male students dominating the conversation—into a positive by asking the two leaders to explain some of their

Student Conversations

Following is a portion of one of our ongoing discussions of shadows on February 4, 1997.

Students are referred to by initials; teacher=T; males= *, females= **.

L*: I think I know how they are made.

T: The shadows?

L*: Uh-huh.

T: Would you like to come on up here and be our second "scientist" then?

[L* positions himself in the middle of the "circle."]

L*: If there was a bright, bright light up here, and it does go like you were talking about [responding to the information C*, the other facilitator, had previously shared], and then you could be right here and you're covering part of the ground and you could be however you want.

C*: I know. That's what I said.

L*: Like if we were outside you can almost always see it on grass.

T: Okay. Have a seat there and you can answer any questions these people have.

C* calls on R*

R*: How, I mean like . . . Why does[n't] it have the color that you have on?

C*: It doesn't.

R*: But why doesn't it?

T: [Clarifying question] Oh, so, why doesn't it have the color that you have on?

C*: It's not really you, it's just . . .

R*: A part of you.

C*: Yeah, it's just a reflection of you.

R*: Oh, okay.

C*: Black on the ground.

L*: Like the Sun, like you're, you're, like you're a dark black cloud.

T: Ooo, we'll have to write a poem about that!

M**: I see a shadow in the room.

T: Oh, you're looking at your shadows in the room?

[Everyone sees shadows on shades with sun shining through the windows. Great excitement! Everyone is talking at once.]

statements. The two became quite humble at some points, saying "I don't know" when asked a question.

At first, the student leaders called on their friends, also male. The naturally quiet students were not as involved at the beginning, but, as time went on, they joined in when called on or when they just wanted to speak. Soon, everyone was participating, both males and females. For the final discussion, when I facilitated, all but one female shared.

One of the questions asked and discussed was "Why doesn't it [the shadow] have the color you have on?" This student wondered why the shadow wasn't the same color as skin. Throughout the discussions, many moments of spontaneous dialog occurred. They were all respectful and involved listeners. Because of the accepting attitude of the group, no laughing or put-downs occurred, even if an idea seemed far-fetched. Some disagreed with statements but were willing to suspend judgment and try to find out for themselves. Spontaneous moments might be seen by some educators as negative, but were some of the more positive moments in my view. They showed that the students were really involved. It was enjoyable to just sit and listen as the children tried to explain their thoughts and communicate their ideas to the group, asking questions of each other for clarification. I planned to have more discussions during the rest of the year, with other students being the leaders.

Learning for All

Questioning techniques can be used by students to learn how to ask questions of themselves or of others to investigate or explore a topic of interest. Questions allow a child to become a leader or teacher as he or she enlarges or guides the discussion in a specific area. I firmly believe that as one teaches, one also learns; thus, children grow in their own skills as they teach others.

Just as questions can help children clarify their own thinking, the teacher can learn much about the students by listening to their discussions. It was very enlightening for me to observe the children's thinking processes as they gave explanations. I also gained insight into class dynamics. During the shadow discussion, the original leaders were male, but in many other subsequent discussions, the females took the lead. I will continue to heighten my awareness of participants in discussions, making a special effort to draw in the "quiet ones" and encourage student leaders to do the same. My goal is to empower the students to have a role in their own education.

Marletta Iwasyk is a kindergarten/first-grade teacher at Orca at Columbia School in Seattle, Washington. Development of this case study was partially supported by the National Science Foundation under grant # MDR-9155726, Emily H. van Zee, Principal Investigator, University of Maryland at College Park.

Resources

Adler, I., and R. Adler. 1961. *Shadows*. New York: John Day.

American Association for the Advancement of Science (AAAS). 1993. *Benchmarks for science literacy*. New York: Oxford University Press.

Asch, F. 1990. *Bear shadow*. New York: Scholastic.

Dorros, A. 1990. *Me and my shadow*. New York: Scholastic.

McDermott, L. 1995. *Physics by inquiry*. New York: J. Wiley.

National Research Council (NRC). 1996. *National Science Education Standards*. Washington, DC: National Academy Press.

Ridiman, R. 1973. What is a shadow? New York: Parents' Magazine Press.

van Zee, E., M. Iwasyk, A. Kurose, D. Simpson, and J. Wild, 1997, February. Teachers as researchers: Studies of student and teacher questions during inquiry-based science instruction. Workshop presented at the annual meeting of the American Association for the Advancement of Science, Seattle, WA.

Also in Science and Children

Bar, V., C. Sneider, and N. Martimbeau. 1997. Teaching Teachers: Is there gravity in space? *Science and Children* 34(7): 38–43.

Padilla, M. J., and E. J. Pyle. 1996. Observing and inferring promotes science learning. *Science and Children* 33(8): 22–25.

Spargo, P. E., and L. G. Enderstein. 1997. Teaching Teachers: What questions do they ask? *Science and Children* 34(6): 43–45.

What the Real Experts Say

My students are just following the Standards and educating me along with themselves.

Carol B. Avila

"But how is this going to lead to lessons that teach the scientific process?"

"What do you mean 'teach the process'?"

"Formulate questions, hypothesize, experiment . . . ." And the science curriculum consultant went through the list like the expert she was. Of course, she taught Methods and Materials of Science Education at the university level; I have first-grade students. I can't teach that fixed set. I can just imagine myself saying, "The students are questioning again when they should be data collecting!" or "Stop that predicting! You haven't even finished designing your experiment!" First-grade students just have no respect for the education expert's sequenced scientific methods.

I left that professional development seminar feeling like a failure—which of course didn't make any sense because, for me, the National Research Council's *National Science Education Standards* (1996) ranks right up there with The Golden Rule and The Bill of Rights. So what is this communication problem many primary school teachers have with science curriculum experts?

It is because we do not know ahead of time what the science lesson will be.

Let the Students Lead

Although primary school teachers use the National Science Education Standards and know what applies, they do not know what the lesson will be. Best-laid plans do not always work for primary grade children. The curriculum director might not know what the lesson will be, and even Bill Nye can't say for sure. Educators have to wait to hear the children's questions that tell the teachers what the students need to know and learn—while the students are messing around with stuff.

One time, the goal of a plant science kit was to demonstrate how plants grew from bulbs. All of the good things for the lesson were in place as our first-grade cooperative groups began to plant tulip bulbs on town land—except that, for safety, I had the students bring flexible plastic rulers instead of our wooden ones.

One group's digger had used a trowel to dig a hole with an estimated depth of 15 cm. The measurer stuck the plastic ruler into the hole hard enough to cause the end of it to curl up. "It's 15!" he called out, although the hole was really little more than half of that.

The student planting the bulb took one look at the ruler curled up at the bottom of the hole and anxiously yelled, "No!" He flapped his arms in frustration and looked to me, "Hey, you can't.... No!" With his head shaking an emphatic negative, he looked back into the hole, at me, at the hole. "Wait it's …."

"Come on, Wally!" the other students called to him.

Wow! This is incredible. Here I have a child who has just turned six, and he is questioning the validity of the measurement process and data.

It was a great opportunity, but the other children weren't ready for me to teach it just then. And Wally sure didn't need it—he had demonstrated his proficiency.

What Wally really needed was to learn how to communicate—he had a language problem. Putting the good stuff in his head into a sentence or two became the lesson. The best support I could give him was time and a few key comments. We were in what Vygotsky (1978) called the *zone of proximal development.*

Ahh, the zone of proximal development … I like that place. Vygotsky believed that real learning was a partnership between adult and student. We keep challenging the children just enough—with questioning and real objects to mess around with—and the students are able to construct knowledge.

I find students are highly entertained by being stretched and required to think. Isn't it just like a human. Below the zone, we bore children; above the zone, we frustrate them. Always, in the zone of proximal development, we support students' thinking. Of course, this kind of learning can't be planned in a planning book; teachers have to know their stuff.

Wally had trouble forming sentences to communicate his ideas, but he didn't need his teacher telling him what to say. He needed to experiment with words and phrases. Communication—the fundamental strand that underlies every content standard—became our lesson.

"Look, Mrs. Avila." He dragged me toward the hole where the measurer with the curled ruler waited and where I could see this big mistake.

"Yes?" I asked innocently. Wally pointed more emphatically and rolled his eyes in exasperation. (I could tell I'd just lost 1,000 points with him, but he had to learn to articulate his ideas.)

"Look it! Look!"

I looked at it with my eyebrows together and a puzzled expression and calmly inquired, "But what is the problem, Wally?"

His eyes were wide, and he emphasized each word with a foot stamp, "It has too many centimeters in a hole!"
(Yyyeeesss!)

Reinventing the Wheel

Like Vygotsky, Eleanor Duckworth (1987) also warned against telling students the answers. Really now, she asked, how much critical thinking goes into merely remembering the right answer?

Not much, but we primary school teachers find that messing around with science and really wondering about "stuff" in a zone of proximal development produces enough brain activity to make a classroom hum like a high-tension wire!

One day a contingent of education specialists (my first-grade students) confronted me as I watched students go out to recess.

"Mrs. Avila," one of them asked as I tied her hood under her chin. "How come we don't do more important science?"

Indeed. Just the day before, a student had spilled some water on his reading response and called everyone over to show us the reds and blues separating out of the black marker. "Cool!" I had said. "I wonder what the purple marker does?" So the children messed around informally with paper chromatography, and later, many shared their research data in our class meeting. It was just another fascinating side trip into how science is always part of our lives. And I was impressed that some children concluded certain colors are "made up of different colors and others, like yellow, seem just plain ol' boring the same."

Now, however, the real curriculum experts were gently criticizing me. They told me that real science happened when I acted important, used science stuff, and talked with big words.

Hmmm. I was about to begin talking about forces and motion; however, Content Standard G, which was nowhere near my lesson plan book, became what the curriculum called for—now.

"Children, gather around. I have to tell you about this person, Newton, who lived around the time of the Pilgrims. He was a famous scientist who …." They loved learning about a wonderer—just like them—who became famous for finding answers to his wonders.

The next day, I commanded a box to "Go into that corner." But, of course, the box didn't move. After the laughter stopped, several students said, "Push it. You have to push it."

"I don't believe it!" I exclaimed. "Who told you that? How do you know that? I don't believe this. I was just going to teach you about a force called *push* and you figured it out. You are thinking science about everyday stuff, the same way Newton did hundreds of years ago! What are you, geniuses?"

We began to design ways to move the box, and it was a glorious adventure in problem solving. "Good grief," I thought one afternoon as the children worked on their Newtonian physics project. "How come they don't know something so obvious?" My mind was racing, and I wasn't sure what I needed to do. Sure enough, the students had invented wheels to make moving the box easier, but they had *taped* them onto the box!

"Why doesn't it wheel?" a group of these first-grade students asked. So I put my chin in my hand and walked around the box saying, "Hmmm." They looked at me. I didn't quite know what they needed, although I was sure it wasn't my telling them, "You need an axle."

"Not tape," said Patti. She was just staring at a taped wheel and said again while shaking her head, "Not tape."

Just before I was about to suggest they go look at other wheels that roll, somebody brought me the big stapler and said, "Staple it right in the middle."

Patti opened her mouth to protest; she guessed it wouldn't work, but I stapled each wheel in the center where the children told me to staple. The tape came off.

Everybody watched.

It didn't roll. Students made exasperated moans and groans and voiced disappointment. The zone of proximal development—wow, we were "ZPDing" at warp speed. Then, the dismissal bell rang.

I knew we needed more fundamental concepts, such as the use of models, on which science knowledge is constructed.

I said to the children, "Detroit is always reengineering their vehicles. The people who make Chevy Corvettes and Ford Mustangs run into these engineering problems all the time. So let's go home and research wheels that work. Look for the ones that roll and make something from materials at home to show us what you find out about wheels that work."

The next morning, the walkers ran all the way to school, and the bus students flew out of their buses as they exploded into the schoolyard with their discoveries. "Look! We need one of these!" one of my students called out to everyone as he displayed a paper towel tube stuck through holes cut in two Cool Whip lids. And the wheels rolled!

"You have to have this!" another student called out as she rolled a pencil stuck through two milk caps. And the wheels rolled!

"Look! I can 'wheel.'" Another student had a piece of vacuum cleaner pipe with an individually wrapped roll of toilet paper on each end. And the wheels rolled!

The Community as a Resource

While the students experimented with wheels and axles, our school received a pamphlet from the Warren Preservation Society inviting community members to participate in the Warren on Wheels Festival. The pamphlet stated that participants could use "anything on wheels—no motors." Using the invitation as an incentive, the children wanted to complete their contraption-that-rolled so they could participate in the festival.

The study of motion had become a study in problem solving and cooperation as the children had continued to build up from wheel and axle. They coached me through all of the hard parts and were very kind about my lack of mechanical insight. This was their project. They brainstormed what needed to be done, pulled apart, reengineered, etc., and expressed gratitude that they had someone like me to do all the "muscle stuff."

In the sunshine of a brilliant June morning, my first-grade students entered their contraption-that-rolled in the annual Warren on Wheels Festival. It seemed as though the whole town was there with balloons, flags, and noisemakers, and the people were all delighted with the schoolchildren and their … um … vehicle.

The vehicle was a three-wheeled box. A round, blue object with a red marker through it made up the front wheel assembly that was attached to the box with pencils and duct tape. Plastic bowls—three each, for strength—with the blackboard pointer through them formed the rear wheel assembly. We had covered the box with streamers, stickers, paint—anything that sparkled, clashed, or made you squint. What a beauty.

The children careened the contraption all over the parade route, calling to each other, laughing, putting plastic bowls back on, putting it right-side-up, and telling dogs, siblings, trees, and curbs to "Get out of the way—we don't have any steering!"

"We won! We won!" The children jumped up and down, enchanting Warren with a display of the town's most valuable resource. The crowd had loved the children and had given them the biggest round of applause. To the students from Main Street School—first prize.

Thus, these young curriculum experts led me through another professional development course—this time in Content Standard G, "Science is not separate from society but rather science is a part of society."

The children demonstrated to me how essential the community is to our classrooms. They wanted to build this thing-on-wheels for their town. The community gave my scientists a purpose, which drove the problem solving and rewarded the perseverance.

What It's All About

The National Research Council states in the *National Science Education Standards*, "There is logic behind the abilities outlined in the inquiry standard, but a step-by-step sequence or scientific method is not implied. In practice, student questions might arise from previous investigations, planned classroom activities, or questions students ask each other" (p. 121).

It is very humbling to see all of that wonderful science that happens in my classroom and know that it wasn't my idea. My students are just following the Standards and educating me along with themselves as they make sense of their world the way scientists do.

Carol B. Avila is a first-grade teacher at Main Street School in Warren, Rhode Island.

Resources

Duckworth, E. 1987. The having of wonderful ideas and other essays on teaching and learning. New York: Teachers College Press.

National Research Council (NRC). 1996. *National Science Education Standards.* Washington, DC: National Academy Press.

Vygotsky, L. S. 1978. *Mind in society.* Cambridge, MA: Harvard University Press.

Also in Science and Children

Hadi-Tabassum, S. 1997. The invention convention: Mind meets simple machines. *Science and Children* 34 (7): 24–27, 47.

Maxim, G. 1997. When to answer the question "Why?" *Science and Children* 35(3): 41–45.

Shiland, T.W. 1997. Decookbook it! *Science and Children* 35 (3): 14–18.

How Big Is Big? How Small Is Small?

We found that our second-grade class did not have an understanding of a giraffe's size.

Lina L. Owens, Fannye E. Love, and Jean M. Shaw

"Wow, this book says a giraffe is 19 feet tall! What would a real giraffe look like?" With this question, prompted by a comment from a student, we found that our second-grade class did not have an understanding of the animal's size.

The children's responses included "Well, it's tall—about as tall as my big brother." "A giraffe is tall as the hospital—that's five stories! It's tall and skinny." "Maybe a giraffe could fit in the gym, but it's too tall to fit in our classroom." "Yes, it could get in our classroom (which had a nine-foot ceiling), but its head would reach the ceiling!"

What the Standards Say

These responses remind us that building understanding of science concepts is an important part of the curriculum as discussed in the *National Science Education Standards* (NRC 1996). According to the Standards, understanding is constructed through individual and social processes. The Teaching Standards emphasize focusing on student understanding and use of scientific knowledge.

Quantification of data and integrating mathematics and science are also emphasized in the Standards. As young students engage in scientific inquiry, they develop the skills to observe, measure, and use tools appropriate for the attributes being measured (i.e., metersticks for length, scales or balances for mass, thermometers for temperature). The Standards further state that students should explore characteristics and structures of organisms and that size is an important characteristic of organisms.

Children are intrigued with the study of animals, and a variety of children's books can be found on this topic. According to the Standards, "It is important for students to learn how to access scientific information from books" (NRC 1996, p. 45). Hamm and Adams (1998) say that "Reading a wide range of texts and literature is a part of science and language learning, giving students new perspectives."

Integrating Literature

We will describe several science trade books that we use with children to build understandings of relative sizes and other measurement concepts. These understandings are then furthered by classroom extensions and investigations.

Biggest, Strongest, Fastest (Jenkins 1995) presents animals that vary greatly in size, speed, and strength. The book features simple statements such as "The tallest animal is the giraffe" and portrays each animal realistically with a collage. Animal records and referents for 14 animals follow in smaller print and smaller silhouette pictures. For the giraffe, the text reads, "Male giraffes grow as tall as 19 feet; the females are a little shorter. With their great height and long, flexible necks, giraffes can eat leaves other grazing animals cannot reach." The last page of the book is a chart that names animals and lists their records, size, diet, and range.

As a classroom follow-up to the reading of the book, pairs of children conduct research on other animals and make similar pages for an original class book. The students make scale drawings using child-size comparisons instead of adult-proportioned ones. This provides students a learning experience and serves as an informal assessment of their abilities to use information about their own heights and heights of animals to draw proportionally. Children approach this task in a variety of ways: Often students depict hippopotamuses and elephants alongside slimmer, shorter pictures of themselves. Some students draw themselves with specklike ants and grasshoppers at their feet. A few picture themselves with their pet dogs and cats, which vary in size,

but are generally shown in realistic proportion to the children's self-portraits.

Using newspaper, yarn, and other inexpensive materials, children create life-size models of some of the animals in the book to capture the scale of the animals described. The models are posted on the classroom walls or displayed in the halls. Students measure and outline large animals' sizes with chalk on outdoor paved surfaces. Children also construct dioramas with humans and animals shown in proportional sizes.

The Big Bug Book (Facklam 1994) highlights animal records, focusing on insects. The book begins with a discussion of relative sizes in the animal kingdom and insects' body parts. The author presents an explanation of size limitations on insects due to their breathing mechanisms. Very large insects would have trouble breathing because insects do not have lungs. Insects get air through small holes in their exoskeleton called *spiracles*. Spiracles are connected with tubes through which air flows to all parts of the insects' body. Thus, no part of an insect's body can be far from its exoskeleton. The book describes 14 insects, including their places of origin, their sizes, and interesting facts about each. Clear, realistic illustrations show each insect in actual size next to common objects such as blocks, crayons, and an apple, thus helping children interpret and comprehend the measurements that are given.

After studying the book's pictures and text, children make their own actual-size drawings of insects and small animals. They select classroom objects such as pencils, markers, and bookmarks, or make an outline of their own hand next to their drawing of an animal to show relative sizes. After dis-

playing the drawings on a bulletin board, we invite another class to view the display and listen to presentations of the project.

Large as Life Animals (Cole 1985) features descriptions and portraits of 20 animals. Each two-page spread of the book shows actual-size animals and includes one or two paragraphs of information about the animals, their habits, and their habitats. Nature Notes, the last eight pages of the book, provides more information and a black-and-white sketch of each featured animal.

A natural extension to *Large as Life Animals* is the compilation of information on more animals. The children work together to make life-size drawings and add measurement data to their descriptions. Large animals are children's favorites for this activity; they often choose to draw dinosaurs such as a *Stegosaurus* or *Triceratops*, or creatures such as rhinoceroses, polar bears, and large snakes. The drawings are then compiled in a class book.

What's Smaller Than a Pygmy Shrew? (Wells 1995) focuses on relative sizes and successively smaller sizes. Encouraging readers to "think small," a 7.5 cm pygmy shrew is compared to a toadstool, an elephant, and a ladybug, emphasizing the idea that the concept of *big* or *small* depends on what objects are being compared. The author then leads readers through thinking about water drops, protozoa that are in the drops, cells that make up the protozoa, bacteria, molecules, atoms, and more. Also included is a discussion of using microscopes to see small objects. The book concludes with a glossary of terms—from *proton* to *quark*.

The book offers information to complement the study of the composition of organisms, as recommended for fifth through

eighth grades in the Standards. After reading the book, students make a panel drawing showing relative sizes and structures of at least four components of living creatures— an entire organism, at least one other organism smaller and one larger than the original, and some of the original organism's cells. Because humans are familiar and pictures of human cells and organs are easy to find in children's reference books, students usually draw people in these panels.

Lifetimes (Rice 1997) takes a different approach than the previously mentioned books by focusing on the life spans of a variety of organisms—from the earthworm (which has a surprisingly long lifetime of six years) to the Venus flytrap to the giant sequoia to the elephant. For each organism included in the book (there are also pages devoted to the Earth, Sun, and universe), there is information about the organism's life span and some interesting facts. Along the bottom of each page is a variety of short directives to the reader. These brief, thought-provoking challenges labeled "Tell About It," "Think About It," "Look It Up," or "Find Out," lead to individual or small group research and sharing of information with the class. The text is enriched with realistic color illustrations that show the organisms and their habitats.

Children use the book's information to begin a database or spreadsheet on organisms, including information on life spans. They also include data on habits and sizes. Some of this information is found in the book, but students also gather research from other sources. Children add creatures and nonliving objects of their choice to the database and organize the information by life span, size, or other categories.

Figure 1. Rubric for Evaluation of Students' Work With Relative Sizes

Excellent (4)
- Student shows unusual understanding of relative sizes.
- Student has independently researched information from more than one source.
- Work is neat, complete, and meaningfully labeled.
- Sharing of information is poised, confident, and complete.

Good (3)
- Student shows understanding of relative sizes.
- Student has researched information from at least one source.
- Work is mostly neat, complete, and meaningfully labeled.
- Sharing of information is clear.

Acceptable (2)
- Student shows some understanding of relative sizes.
- Student research is gained from others.
- Parts of work are neat, complete, and labeled.
- Sharing of information is clear after prompting.

Needs Improvement (1)
- Student shows little understanding of relative sizes.
- Work shows little or no research.
- Work lacks neatness, completeness, and labeling.
- Sharing of information is not clear, even after prompting.

Assessment

When children complete the extension activities, there are many opportunities to use ongoing assessment, oral explanations, and students' critiques of their own work as recommended in the Standards. We have found that, typically, much conversation and informal peer-assessment occurs as children complete and share the extension activities. We sometimes give the children daily credit/daily grades or ask them to write about their work in journals or on papers that are then attached to the students' drawings and other products.

Keeping the following questions in mind, we also informally assess children's learning as they present their results within small or large groups:

- Do the children seem to understand what they are showing and talking about?
- Do their gestures and drawings convey information?
- Can the children compare their information to objects in the classroom and other familiar referents?

In addition, we have developed a simple rubric (Figure 1) for assessment of students'

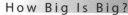

work; we use this rubric occasionally to evaluate products for credit.

The Long and Short of It

Using literature and follow-up activities greatly helps children construct understanding and appreciation of measurement concepts as they apply to science. Many factual books are available that can be used for large group instruction as well as displayed in centers for individual and small group use. (See *Science and Children*'s "Outstanding Science Trade Books for Children" list, published annually in the March issue and available on *Science and Children*'s homepage at *www.nsta.org/pubs/sc.*)

Perhaps the next time a student says, "A giraffe is as tall as the trees on the playground," he or she just might be correct thanks to a teacher who helped the student construct the concept of sizes.

Lina L. Owens is an assistant professor of education, Fannye E. Love is an associate professor of education, and Jean M. Shaw is a professor of education, all at the University of Mississippi–Oxford.

Resources

Hamm, M., and Adams, D. 1998. Reaching across disciplines (What research says). *Science and Children* 36 (1): 45–49.

National Research Council (NRC). 1996. *National Science Education Standards*. Washington, DC: National Academy Press.

Outstanding science trade books for children for 1999. 1999. *Science and Children* 37 (6): 17–23.

Recommended Children's Books

Cole, J. 1985. *Large as life animals*. Paintings by K. Lilly. New York: Alfred A. Knopf.

Facklam, M. 1994. *The big bug book*. Illustrated by P. Facklam. Boston: Little, Brown.

Jenkins, S. 1995. *Biggest, strongest, fastest*. New York: Ticknor & Fields.

Rice, D. L. 1997. *Lifetimes*. Illustrated by M.S. Maydak. Nevada City, CA: Dawn Publications.

Wells, R. E. 1995. *What's smaller than a pygmy shrew?* Morton Grove, IL: Albert Whitman.

Also in Science and Children

Anshutz, R. J., P. L. Callison, and E. L. Wright, (1997. Gummy worm measurement. *Science and Children* 35 (1): 38–41.

Eagles, C. 1994. Mad for metric measure. *Science and Children* 31 (4): 23–25, 59.

Sherman, H. J. 1997. Sizing up the metric system. *Science and Children* 35 (2): 27–31.

Child-Centered Curricula

The Bird

The children learned … that real science is wondering, searching, and wondering some more.

Jean Hannon

SAFETY NOTE

Please be aware of the necessary safety and health precautions—gloves, protective clothing, hand washing, and possibly masks—needed for this or any similar activity, particularly with young children. In this article, the author continuously reminds the children not to touch, but only observe the bird. Adults involved in such an activity need to model the precautions necessary when handling animal specimens as these professionals did. Also, some states have regulations regarding the handling of wildlife. Contact your state's department of health or a local animal control center to find out those that apply where you live.

I almost missed the bird. If it had been three years earlier, before I began my studies in early childhood education as part of a master's program through the University of Alaska–Southeast, I would have completely ignored the teaching opportunities its death granted. As it was, I had to remind myself of the importance of child-centered learning.

Alex and Sam, two students in my kindergarten class, found the bird on the playground near the bench. Excitedly they asked me to come and look. A group of children gathered around the stiff, feathered body. Anna thought its tail looked like that of a grouse. Amanda thought that the bird was "very pretty"; many children commented on

the beauty of its tail feathers. (The bird was preserved by several −45°C days and nights. February temperatures in interior Alaska can dip quite low for extended periods of time.)

We picked up the motionless bird with a snow shovel and brought it into the classroom. I discussed with the children the importance of not touching the bird with either their mittened or bare hands because of the possibility of contracting a disease from bacteria on the bird's body. The children complied.

What Should We Do With It?

The children sat around the bird and suggested possibilities: bury it, throw it in the garbage, let it stay outside, watch it, put it in a container in the sun, let it sleep inside, ask a doctor or the school nurse for help, put it in hot water. I wrote each suggestion on chart paper.

Most children thought that there was still hope for the bird. Austin suggested that it was tired and was covering its eyes with its wings. Janice thought the bird had been flying around, got kicked by another bird, and fell down. Sara said that we should let the bird rest, "then it would get alive."

Jim was one of the few students to discuss death. He said that maybe the bird had been shot, had frozen, or had died because of the actions of some other animal like a bear.

Although Jim agreed that the bird might be dead, he suggested resuscitating it. "How do you spell CPR?" he asked quietly, during a chance moment when we were alone. With my prompting, he carefully added his offering to the class suggestion list.

The children were pleased with their list. Because I simply thanked each child who volunteered an idea, they understood that each recommendation was equally valuable.

The Nurse Visits

Following one of the ideas on the list, we asked Mrs. Birch, our school nurse, to inspect the bird. The children watched intently as she made a thorough examination. Mrs. Birch wore disposable gloves the entire time, and she repeated to the children the importance of not touching the bird without "nurse gloves." She gradually led the children to understand that the bird was dead and beyond saving.

"Mrs. Birch said that when birds are in the winter for a long time, they get cold," said Katie.

"The bird died out in the snow," continued Luke. "It got too frozen."

William seemed to understand that some birds migrate in the winter. He said, "I think the snow made it die. It should have gone somewhere else with the other birds."

The children also learned from Mrs. Birch's comments that some animals die naturally from old age: "It was too tired," said Dylan. "It didn't have enough breath anymore. It was flying too long."

"Maybe it was 20 years old, and it died," Jody guessed.

Later Jenny commented, "Mrs. Birch is good at looking at birds."

"Yes," agreed Adam. "The nurse treats animals and people very good."

At this point, most of the students understood and accepted the bird's death. We talked with Mr. Walker, Brandon's dad, who was working with us that day. He suggested either taxidermy or placing the bird back in the woods that bordered our school's playground. After some discussion, the students wanted to place the bird back in the woods. Many of the children, despite expert advice, still hoped that the bird would come alive in the spring.

Back to the Woods

We invited a school parent, who was a local forest ranger, to come to our class and tell us what might happen if the bird was placed back in the woods. Since the outdoor temperatures remained below zero, we kept the bird in a covered box outside our classroom door while we waited the two days for the forest ranger to visit our classroom.

The forest ranger, Mrs. Everett, discussed what might have happened to the bird.

One student said, "Mrs. Everett taught us about the bird and about other animals. She said it might have frozen. She told us that if we put it back in the wilderness, other animals can use the feathers and bones for their nests so they can survive in the cold."

"Mrs. Everett told us that we could let the other animals eat the bird. We could keep it in the woods. We could let squirrels eat it. We could let the little birds have parts of it," added Kyle.

On another sheet of chart paper, I listed how the bird could be used if it was placed in the woods. With time and discussion, we came to an agreement: "If we put the bird back in nature," Elton said, "animals can eat it."

The forest ranger led us on a path into the woods. I carried the bird on a piece of cardboard from its "storage" box. Under the gaze of the silent students, Mrs. Everett took the bird, walked off the path a short distance, and slid the bird from the cardboard onto the snow.

"We put the bird back in the woods so that little birds and other little animals could use it," said Alex. "Mrs. Everett went a little ways alone so the little animals would not be afraid of our smell. Mrs. Everett taught us a lot about animals."

In a fitting eulogy, Anna said, "We gave the bird back to life."

Over the next few days, the children wondered aloud about the bird. They also shared stories of pets that had died. A few children talked about the possibility of a heaven or other afterlife. I encouraged the students to talk with their families about these concepts and concerns.

What Will We See?

Three months later, with the snow and cold gone from the boreal forests of interior Alaska, our class followed the same path to the place where we had left the bird. Before going, I reviewed with the class the charts we had written earlier, and the children suggested possibilities of what we might find in that area: feathers, bones, the whole bird, or nothing. We found nothing.

"What do you think happened?" I asked.

"A moose took it," said Jeremy. He was not discouraged a bit when another child mentioned that moose generally ate plants.

"The little animals pulled pieces of it into their tunnels," said Patricia, who seemed to remember our discussion with the forest ranger.

For a short time longer the children searched the forest floor for evidence of the bird and because they were five- and six-year-old children who had just endured seven months of winter, the children's investigations shifted to the new growth around them.

As I watched them, I attempted to elaborate for myself what the children had learned from the death of one bird. The children had grown in their abilities to take part in a group, to listen, to work toward consensus, and to respect another's ideas. The children may have also learned something about the life cycle, the food chain, the significant contributions an animal can make to its habitat, and the concept that little is wasted in nature. Most important, perhaps, the children learned that they could hypothesize and then look for answers and that real science is wondering, searching, and wondering some more.

Jean Hannon teaches kindergarten at Badger Road Elementary in Fairbanks, Alaska.

Gravitating Toward Reggio

The children's predictions lay the foundation for observations, discussions, and explorations.

Josephine M. Shireen DeSouza and Jill Jereb

Reggio Emilia, a city in northern Italy, has become famous worldwide for its preprimary school education. The quality of this educational program has received much attention and accolades from early childhood educators around the world (Gandini 1997).

The Reggio Emilia Approach has a unique composition of educational elements. One such element is the emergent unplanned curriculum. The teacher elicits ideas from children and channels the curriculum through long-term projects. The children's predictions lay the foundation for many observations, discussions, and explorations that take place during the course of the project. The teacher scaffolds ideas to sustain the interest and learning, perpetuating a continuous dialogue among teachers and children (Gandini, 1997).

Bringing Forth the Idea

A former kindergarten teacher acquaintance of mine learned about the Reggio Emilia Approach through a workshop at her school. Her experiences with the emergent curriculum began when the classroom computer began to have audio problems. The children asked her to fix it, but she explained that she did not know how to fix a computer.

The students were not happy with this answer, so she asked them what they thought she could do. They suggested that she: "Just go inside and fix it." "Turn up the volume." "Turn it off and on." and "Put in a different game." The teacher tried some of these, and nothing helped. She told the students that a computer repairperson would have to be called. Reflecting on this experience, she thought it would be fun and educational to explore machines and how they work.

Structuring the Environment

The following day during circle time, the teacher gathered the children on the carpet. On chart paper, students drew a web with the word *machines* in the center and, as a group, shared what they already knew about machines. The teacher wrote a list as the children named machines, the objects they make, and how lives are made easier by using machines. They also discussed machine parts and the sounds they make.

Later, the children drew and wrote about their favorite machine(s) in their science journals. They drew pictures of machines they thought they could live without and an invented machine that would make their lives easier.

Instructors and children can go in any direction at this point in this unit. This kindergarten class focused on simple machines—the kind that don't use electrical power or gasoline.

May the Force Be With You

The kindergarten teacher asked the children to look around the classroom and explain what things were moving, how they were moving, and how fast they were moving. Everyone found something in the room that could move on its own and something that needed help. Some examples included the clock, the fish in the aquarium, and the chair on rollers.

Topic: Simple machines
at *www.scilinks.org*
code: SC400a

Topic: Force
at *www.scilinks.org*
code: SC400b

The students started moving things around in different ways. Some worked together to move heavy objects while others pushed, pulled, picked up, and blew things around. Through their interactions with the objects, they discovered that a lot of factors determine what moves, how it moves, and how fast it moves. They soon learned that almost everything moves because of the power of *force*, which causes an object to move, stop, or change directions. The children discovered many concepts involving force: "It doesn't take much force to move these books." "My body is a force." "It is a lot easier when we do it together." "Is wind a force?"

On another day, the teacher asked the children if they thought they could lift one of their friends using their own strength. The students all assured her that they could. They were then asked if they could lift two of their friends. Most said no. The teacher told them that if they constructed a simple machine called a lever they could even lift her.

After hearing this, the children used two-by-fours and blocks of wood to experiment with the design of a lever. They made seesaws, lifted up objects, and experimented with different lengths of planks and different sizes and positions of the fulcrum. Soon they were lifting each other and the teacher with only the force of one of their arms. Students discovered that where they placed the fulcrum determined how easily they could force a person up. The children's comments included: "It is easy with the lever." "This is like a seesaw." "He made the basket fall over because he jumped on the lever."

What Goes Up …

During the second week of exploration, students experimented with forces such as gravity, friction, inertia, and centrifugal force. They conducted experiments involving gravity, such as dropping balls of various weights and sizes simultaneously from different heights. They predicted that the heavier, larger balls would drop to the floor faster than the smaller, lighter ones. Much to their amazement, they observed that the balls landed on the floor at the same time when dropped from the same height, and they recorded this discovery in their journals.

Students also used ramps and cars at different angles to demonstrate gravitational pull. Through their observations they discovered that gravity is the force that pulls things toward the ground.

This experimentation led them to investigate another important force called friction. "Why do your cars always go farther than our cars?" one child asked as he observed the other group playing with ramps and cars. The teacher asked, "What do you think is happening?" After a short discussion, someone said that it was the carpet. "Carpet slows things down." "The smooth floor makes the cars go farther and faster." "The cars go faster when the ramp is higher up." "Gravity is pulling them down." In reaction to this discussion, the teacher asked if anyone knew what friction was. No one could describe it, yet they had all seen it in action.

The discussion of friction continued, and the children came up with another experiment to reduce friction or increase it. With a stationary bike brought into the classroom, everyone had a chance to experiment with the brakes. The children discovered the force of inertia when they peddled the cycle. "What is the force that makes the wheel turn?" the teacher asked. There was unanimous response—it was the force of their leg muscles. "Why didn't the wheel stop when you stopped peddling?" she asked. "Because it is going too fast." "We didn't make it stop." "It has to run out of force." They were told this force had a name: *inertia*, a force that does not have to be constant for the object to keep moving. The next day everyone went to the playground and discovered inertia on swings, merry-go-rounds, bicycles, and scooters.

Centripetal force was briefly covered the last day of experimentation. The teacher prompted the children with a question, "Can we keep water in a bucket even if we turn it upside down?" None of the children believed it could happen, so the teacher gave it a try. She showed them how to spin the bucket and then added water.

The students spun it fast, slow, and in-between. After everyone got the hang of it , they conducted a test to see who could spin the bucket the slowest and not lose the water. The competition was intense, and everyone ended up getting wet, which prompted the question, "Why did the water pour out?"

The children vaguely understood the forces on the water. When the spinning became too slow, the force of gravity was greater than the centripetal force needed to keep the water in orbit, so it accelerated the water down. The water spilled out when gravity took over. This was the hardest concept for children to understand.

In Step With the Standards

During this activity the children wrote, read, counted, built vocabulary, and developed

Connecting to the Standards

Reflecting upon the Reggio Emilia Approach and justifying its pertinence to this activity, one can clearly observe the correlation between the recommendations of the National Science Education Standards and the opportunities these young children were provided to learn science.

Science as Inquiry Content Standard A—As a result of the activities in grades K–4, all students should develop abilities necessary to do scientific inquiry and understandings about scientific inquiry.

The project centered on children's questions about forces. In their quest to know, they constructed knowledge about ideas such as inertia, friction, and gravity through systematic observations of their actions on objects. As they communicated with each other and their teacher, they exchanged ideas and proposed explanations that were documented in their journals.

Physical Science Content Standard B—As a result of the activities in grades K–4, all students should develop an understanding of position and motion of objects.

The children discovered some important facts about applying forces to objects. In a comparison of how far their cars traveled, students were able to infer that the greater the force applied, the farther the car traveled. They also observed that the distance the car traveled on the smooth floor was greater than on the carpeted floor. The word *friction* was introduced to them. The effect gravity had on objects was demonstrated through simple investigations.

science and social skills. Force and motion concepts were easily learned by capturing children's interests and having them answer their own questions. The whole process evolved and took the direction chosen by the children. Learning just happens!

According to the National Research Council recommendation, "When students describe and manipulate objects by pushing, pulling, throwing, dropping, and rolling, they also begin to focus on the position and movement of objects: describing location as up, down, in front, or behind, and discovering the various kinds of motion and forces required to control it" (NRC 1996, p. 126).

Even though force, inertia, gravity, and friction are all separate concepts, young children can recognize that all of these forces act together in a system. In using the Reggio Emilia Approach, children's natural curiosity, thirst for knowledge, and interests in the world around them are sustained and nurtured. The nature of these activities is open-ended and child centered. The teacher and the children are co-constructors of knowledge, which creates a successful learning atmosphere.

The Reggio Emilia Approach allows for parental involvement. This project invited parents to contribute old machines that children investigated and disassembled. Through documenting their own work—with photographs, journal writing, transcriptions of children's discussions, explanations, and comments—during several stages of the project, children were motivated to learn and can see for themselves the progress they have made.

Parents become more aware of their child's experience at school, which gives them an opportunity to suggest ways in which they can contribute to further learning either during a field trip or in the classroom. Teachers can benefit from the opportunity to examine their own role in this teaching-learning process and gain an insight into the teaching process.

Young children need to experience science in such a way that they are excited about what they are doing and are engaged in building ideas, giving explanations, and constructing knowledge through developing science process skills.

Josephine M. Shireen DeSouza is an assistant professor in the Department of Biology at Ball State University, and Jill Jereb is a teacher with the Muncie Public Schools, both in Muncie, Indiana.

Resources

Edwards, C., L. Gandini, and G. Forman, eds. 1993. *The hundred languages of children: The Reggio Emilia approach to early childhood education.* Norwood, NJ: Ablex.

Gandini, L. 1997. The foundations of the Reggio Emilia Approach. In ed. J. Hendrick, *First steps towards teaching the Reggio way,* 14–23. Upper Saddle River, NJ: Prentice Hall.

National Research Council (NRC). 1996. *National Science Education Standards.* Washington, DC: National Academy Press.

Also in Science and Children

Avila, C. 1998. What the real experts say. *Science and Children* 35 (7): 14–17, 42.

Iwasyk, M. 1997. Kids questioning kids: Experts sharing. *Science and Children* 35 (1): 42–46, 80.

Rule, A., and M. T. Barrera, 1999. Science object boxes. *Science and Children* 37 (2): 30–35, 63.

Spiderrific Learning Tools

Explore the creepy-crawly world of spiders with a hands-on activity even an arachnophobe will love.

Kevin J. Mitchell and Keith G. Diem

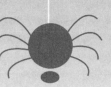

"Eeek ... a spider!" Often, adults' and children's reactions to an identical event yield opposite results. While the sight of a spider may cause a shriek of alarm from an adult, the very same sight might evoke a squeal of delight and fascination from a child. Even icky and gross creatures can become part of great science lessons. That's the goal of Spiderrific, a unit of the New Jersey 4-H Science Discovery Series. This curriculum capitalizes on the notion that broader science concepts can be learned from "teachable moments" with real-world creatures and settings.

As presenter and creator of this 4-H unit in Wayne, New Jersey, we have visited classrooms, after-school programs, camps, county fairs, and 4-H Clubs to dispel myths about spiders. This article describes one of our successful spider lessons in which students get caught in the web of these amazing arachnids.

Spiders Versus Insects

Spiders are invertebrate animals found throughout the world. Many people incorrectly think spiders are insects. Insects and spiders both belong to the same phylum, *Arthropoda*. However, insects belong to the class *Insecta*, and spiders belong to the class *Arachnida*. Insects have three pairs of legs and three body parts: head, thorax, and abdomen. All spiders have the following basic characteristics:

- Two body parts: the *cephalothorax* and the *abdomen*,
- Four pairs of legs, and
- *Spinnerets* located on the abdomen.

There are more than 37,000 species of spiders divided into three groups: primitive spiders, tarantulas, and true spiders. Primitive spiders have segmented abdomens, live in burrows in the ground, and are found only in East Asia. The familiar, hairy tarantulas have jaws on the front of their cephalothorax that move up and down parallel to each other. They are found in the tropical and sub-

Figure 1. Types of Spider Webs.

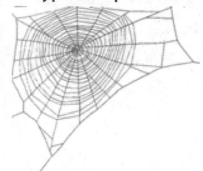

Orb Web—The shape most people think of when they think of spider webs. A wheel-like web suspended between plants, trees, etc. that contains threads that spiral from the middle to the outer edge of web.

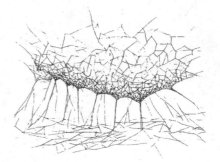

Sheet Web—The main part of the web is composed of closely woven threads and the web is usually oriented horizontally.

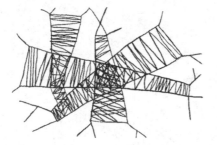

Funnel Web—This web is similar to the sheet web except for a funnel shape that descends from one part of the web. The spider usually "hides" in this funnel waiting for an insect to fall into the web.

Cobweb—An irregular web made of a mass of threads going in all directions.

Diagrams of spider webs reproduced or adapted with permission of the publisher: *Hands-on Nature,* Vermont Institute of Natural Science.

tropical regions of the world. In the United States, tarantulas can be found west of the Mississippi River as far north as central California. True spiders are the most commonly encountered and include orb weavers, wolf spiders, jumping spiders, funnel web spiders, and crab spiders.

Spiders are well-known for weaving webs. Silk glands inside the abdomen produce silk for weaving webs and for other purposes—to catch prey, wrap prey for stor-

age, wrap and protect eggs, make a shelter, use as a safety rope when climbing, and for *ballooning* (floating on the wind). Spiders make different types of silk for different uses—some sticky and some not so sticky. The silk passes through the *spinnerets*, which control the amount of silk used in making the silk threads.

Not all spiders weave webs. Some spiders (wolf spiders, jumping spiders, and fishing spiders) stalk or ambush their prey. Crab spiders wait in ambush to capture unsuspecting insects. Where a spider lives affects how it makes its web. Several different types of spider webs are shown in Figure 1. Typically, a spider that lives in the basement of a house would make a *cobweb*. Some spiders that live in a garden would make *orb webs*. Most people have seen an orb web—especially if they know the story of *Charlotte's Web* (White 1974).

Most spiders pose no danger to humans and are in fact beneficial, eating millions of insects each year. Although few spiders are able to bite through human skin, some North American spiders—such as the black widow and the brown recluse—can be dangerous and their bites can be quite serious. Warn students against handling unidentified spiders.

Do, Reflect, and Apply

The New Jersey 4-H Science Discovery Series (see "Internet Resources") uses a multistep process of experiential learning—*do, reflect, and apply*—to explore science topics. Experiential learning (learning by doing) is just that—learning from experiences. Instead of being told the answers, students are presented with a problem, situation, or activity which they must make sense of for themselves with limited guidance from a teacher. This learning approach was developed in 1992 by the Extension Service of the United States Department of Agriculture and is an essential component of all 4-H programs and curricula.

Not every step of the do, reflect, and apply process is done for every activity, and sometimes steps within each of the three are combined. It is important, however, for students to experience all of the three main processes of the learning cycle by the time the activity is finished. The activities are designed to be action-oriented and require students to work together in groups to make observations, analyze their observations, and arrive at justifiable conclusions through consensus.

The Spiderrific curriculum was designed for grades 4–6, but children as young as four and five years of age have participated in the web activity at after-school and library programs. The Spiderrific unit includes the following lessons:

- Insect or Arachnid?—introduces the characteristics of insects and arachnids;
- Miss Muffet Was Misinformed—explains why students should not be afraid of spiders;
- How to Become a Spider Detective—covers the basic needs of an organism to survive; this information is then used to locate spiders;
- Observing a Spider's Dinner Table—explains the eating habits of spiders and differences between an herbivore and a carnivore;
- Sensitive Spiders Sensing Swaying Webs—teaches students how spiders determine when something is caught in their web;
- Houdini Spider—introduces techniques spiders use to prevent them from getting caught in their own webs; and,
- If You Were a Spider, What Kind of Web Would You Spin?

As students participate in the unit activities they not only discover interesting facts, such as insects and spiders are different from each other, but also re-discover information they already knew, such as spiders spin webs, but not all webs are the same, reinforcing their learning experience.

Spinning a Web

Through the activity If You Were a Spider, What Kind of Web Would You Spin?, students learn about the basic types of spider webs and how the designs of these webs affect their functions while experiencing the three stages of experiential learning.

To begin, I review with students that spiders are *predators* and *carnivores*. I ask the class if they know of any animals that eat other animals. Usually several students respond that they have seen lions eating zebras or snakes eating mice on television or in movies. I explain that the lions and snakes are *carnivores* because they eat meat. I also explain that because lions and snakes sneak up on and catch the animals they want to eat, the lions and snakes are also called *predators*.

Next, we discuss what spiders eat (insects and sometimes other spiders) and how they catch their prey (stalking their prey like a lion or trapping their prey using a web). Students often surprise me with such insightful questions as, "Do spiders eat only one kind of insect?" "Do spiders ever leave their web to look for insects?" and "Why do some spiders eat other spiders?" It's helpful to have field guides or other books available for the extra curious (see "Resources").

The different types of spider webs (see Figure 1) are then shown to the class and discussed. I explain to students that they will be working in teams of two or three to construct spider webs. Students are usually so excited about designing and constructing their own spider webs that they want to start right away. I ask the students, "If you were real spiders, how would you know if your web was a good web?" Several students respond, "It catches bugs or insects!" Then I

explain how each group will have their web tested by tossing a ping-pong ball pseudo-insect representing their prey at the web to see if it gets caught in the web.

To complete this activity, you'll need about an hour and the following materials:

- Ping-pong balls (one or two per class);
- Various kinds and sizes of string and tape—masking tape and single-sided or double-sided transparent tape;
- Notepad and pen or pencil—for taking notes and/or designing their web before students build it;
- Pictures of spider web types; and
- Frames—purchased or homemade—of various sizes to use as templates for making webs. Frames can be constructed from a mason lath (a piece of wood approximately 4 ft. long, 1.5 in. wide, and 0.5 in. thick available at hardware and lumber stores). I use a wooden frame because it is durable and can be reused many times, but cardboard could also be used to make frames.

Caught in the Web

After our discussion about spiders, we begin the "Do" phase of the activity. I tell each group to pretend they are spiders and construct a web to catch a pseudo-insect using the frames and various kinds of string and tape.

Students really like this part of the activity because it allows them to share ideas and to be creative. While the students are constructing their webs, I walk around the classroom to give them encouragement and see if they have questions or need help. If they ask how to build the web, I briefly review with them the webs we discussed earlier and encourage them to be creative and do the best they can to work together to construct a web that will catch the pseudo-insect.

Some students try to copy the design of real spider webs; some students get creative and blend the designs of the spider webs; and some students try to complete the task as quickly as possible by wrapping the frame with only tape or string. I ask these students if they think a spider would be able to produce that much silk to make the type of web they designed. Younger students often need help cutting the string or tape and sometimes expect the teacher to tell them the best way to make the web. When I explain to them that they are the spiders, however, they create unique webs.

Throughout the activity, I write terms, such as *insect*, *spider*, *cephalothorax*, *predator*, *carnivore*, *cobweb*, and *orb web*, on the board for review and to help students with pronunciation and spelling.

Web Testing

Finally, I ask each group to explain its web design and why they think it will be successful. Students can't wait to show off their creations and see if it will catch the "pseudo-insect." They hold the web steady when the ping-pong ball is tossed towards the web. Some get caught in the web and some go right through or bounce off. When a pseudo-insect is caught, the whole class erupts with excitement—students are amazed that there is not just one correct way to build a web. Now it is time for the "reflect" step. Each group compares its web designs with the web designs of the other groups to determine how the designs affected the ability of the web to catch the pseudo-insect.

We also make comparisons to the real types of spider webs. Some, but not all, stu-

dents realize what the string and tape represent: string represents the nonsticky threads of the web, and tape represents the sticky threads of the web. When students make these observations, the students that used only string in their web designs and those that wrapped their frames with tape without any of the sticky part exposed discover why they didn't catch anything in their webs. If students do not make this connection, I ask them if they have ever seen real spider webs, walked into a spider web, or seen an insect caught in a real spider web. Students usually talk about how the webs are sticky and how there must be nonsticky threads on the web too because the spiders do not get caught in their own web.

In the third step of applying their new knowledge, I ask the students how they could improve their web designs. Their conclusions typically include using more tape and less string and making the web less rigid so the pseudo-insect is more likely to get caught and not bounce off the web. I also explain that students should not be discouraged because spiders usually spend more time making webs than they did, and spiders do not catch every insect in their web.

What Do Students Think?

The learning doesn't have to stop here. For follow-up experiences in the classroom, we recommend teachers ask students to explain what they think would be the best design, and why, for a spider web in a garden, in the basement of a house, in a lawn, and so on. Other activities could include being a spider detective by searching for spider webs and observing what is on the spider's dinner table, the web. Students can then observe how

Connecting to the Standards

This article relates to the following *National Science Education Standards* (NRC 1996):

Content Standards
Grades K–4

Unifying Concepts and Processes
- Evidence, models, and organization
- Form and function

Standard A: Science as Inquiry
- Abilities necessary to do scientific inquiry
- Understandings about scientific inquiry

Standard C: Life Science
- The characteristics of organisms
- Organisms and environments

Standard E: Science and Technology
- Abilities of technological design

many insects are in the web, what kinds of insects they are, and hypothesize how the design and location of the web affect the kinds of insects caught in the web.

The Spiderrific unit has been a big hit with boys and girls in grades one through six. Students were interested to learn about the anatomy of a spider and will use this new information when encountering spiders and insects. A few students told me they may even consider becoming an entomologist.

Kevin J. Mitchell (Mitchell@aesop.rutgers.edu) *is a County 4–H Agent at the Rutgers Cooperative Extension of Sussex County in Newton, New Jersey. Keith G. Diem* (Kdiem@aesop.rutgers.edu) *is a program leader in educational design at the Department of 4–H Youth Development at Rutgers University in New Brunswick, New Jersey.*

Resources

Antonelli, A. L. 1997. *Insect answers: Spiders.* Puyallup, WA: Washington State University Cooperative Extension.

Baird, C. R., H. W. Homan, and J. P. McCaffrey. 1993. *Spiders and their relatives.* Moscow, ID: University of Idaho College of Agriculture Cooperative Extension System Agricultural Experiment Station.

Borror, D. J., and R. E. White. *The Peterson field guide series: A field guide to insects, American north of Mexico.* Boston: Houghton Mifflin.

Diem, K. 2001. Turn any science topic into hands-on fun. *Science Scope* 24 (7): 46–49.

Diem, K. et al. 2000. *New Jersey 4–H science discovery series vol. 2.* New Brunswick, NJ: Rutgers University—New Jersey Agricultural Experiment Station.

Levi, H. W., and L. R. Levi. 1987. *Spiders and their kin.* New York: Golden.

Lingelbach, J., and L. Purcell. 2000. *Hands on nature: Information and activities for exploring the environment with children.* Woodstock, VT: Vermont Institute of Natural Science.

Milne, L., and M. Milne. 1990. *The Audubon Society field guide to North American insects and spiders.* New York: Knopf.

National Research Council (NRC). 1996. *National Science Education Standards.* Washington, DC.: National Academy Press.

White, E. B. 1974. *Charlotte's web.* New York: Harper Trophy.

Internet Resources

Rutgers Cooperative Extension New Jersey 4–H Science Discovery Series *www.discoverscience.rutgers.edu*

Southwest Educational Development Laboratory: Spiders *www.sedl.org/scimath/pasopartners/spiders/welcome.html*

It's a Frog's Life

We chose to share this story because it is an exemplary article about real inquiry. —Chris Ohana, *Science and Children* editor

Audrey L. Coffey and Donna R. Sterling

As the owner, director, and head teacher of a small preschool that serves three- to five-year-old children, my main interest is discovering the wonders of the world with my students. Many early childhood educators extol the virtues of water play for this age, and I am no exception. To teach observation skills, cause and effect, volume, properties of water, and more, there's no substitute for that magical substance we call H_2O.

In my school our water table is a sturdy blue baby pool—with a drain—that sits outside on a gravel circle on the playground. After we provide buckets, sieves, cups, funnels, and large plastic aprons, and seasonal changes occur, water can provide endless learning experiences and—as I discovered quite unexpectedly one summer day—can be the source of a teachable moment too good to pass up.

What Is *That*?

Teachable moments are just that—moments a teacher can use spontaneously to add to students' life experiences and enrich their learning. I experienced one last August as my students and I clustered around our pool on water center day. To my dismay, the pool cover had been left off the previous night. "What's that?," children asked as they pointed at something in the pool. "Oh, just some bugs that landed in the water overnight," I quickly answered, my mind preoccupied with the task of draining and cleaning the pool. "What's *that*?," they asked again, still pointing. This time, I stopped to look. There, floating in several jellylike masses were little, black, round . . . eggs. What a teaching moment! I immediately called the class together and explained they were *frogspawn*, or eggs. The children loved the word *spawn*. They loved the eggs. Immediately, they wanted to know what would hatch from the eggs.

When I answered "tadpoles" and saw their expressions, I knew I would not be draining the pool any time soon. It had turned into a frog pond overnight. As we went back indoors, my brain was humming with the implications: fitting real-life learning experiences into our curriculum, safety, and logistics.

A Note From *the Science and Children* Editor

I was captivated by this article the first time I read it. It captures the essence of inquiry. The children and the teachers had a serendipitous encounter with an unknown. The teacher and students worked together to unravel the mystery and discover that the coolest possible thing happened: They had frogs! They then went about researching, studying, and observing the eggs as they changed to tadpoles and then frogs.

As we re-read the article and consulted with the NSTA Safety Committee, some concerns emerged. What are the safety issues with keeping a wading pool in a preschool? What pathogens might lurk in the murky water? What about mosquitoes? What might be the consequences of handling for the frogs? For the children? The most simple and elegant of lessons—kids and frogs—is riddled with potential risks for amphibians and humans alike.

Granted, this experience isn't likely to be replicated, but because of the safety and health concerns associated with it, we are taking the opportunity to offer the following guidelines and suggestions when studying live animals or plants:

- Know all the possible risks. Make sure that children wash their hands thoroughly after handling any animal. There are obvious dangers with wading pools and small children. Drowning is one, and water kept more than a few days can harbor increasing colonies of bacteria. These bacteria can be passed to children as they dip their hands into the water and proceed to put a finger or two into their mouths. They need not drink it to ingest it.

- One solution would be to remove the eggs from the pool and bring them to an indoor aquarium, allowing you to change the pool water every few days without disturbing the frogs. If you remove the eggs (see next bullet), be sure you know what the organisms require.

- Leave the animal or plant as undisturbed as possible. If an animal (or plant) must be brought indoors, be sure to know its requirements first. Consult someone from a department of natural resources or a comparable expert to learn about the needs of the animal and if keeping it is advisable. If you cannot identify the animal by species, resist the temptation to bring it indoors.

- Minimize or eliminate physical contact with the animal. Frogs have very sensitive skin. Soap residues or lotions can kill frogs or make them ill. Amphibian skin must also stay moist, so any time they are handled, hands should be wet. Unfortunately, this leads to slippery frogs that may become airborne and potentially flattened.

- Please consult the NSTA guidelines and your district policy on safety before keeping any classroom pet or animal.

We chose to share this story because it is an exemplary article about real inquiry. It is also a cautionary tale about supervising this type of naturalistic investigation and serves as a study in how to protect all of the creatures involved. With these considerations in mind, we encourage teachers to investigate the natural world with children.

Now, enjoy the wonder of these preschool students as they embark on this surprising inquiry experience.

—*Chris Ohana*

NSTA Connection

The NSTA guidelines for working with animals in the classroom are available in *Safety in the Elementary Science Classroom* (Kwan and Texley 2002).

Standing by my new pond that afternoon, I realized I knew very little about frogs. I knew I'd have to do my homework (research) to create and plan age-appropriate learning experiences for my students, and I knew I'd have to identify the skills I wanted them to master. Right away, I thought of observation skills. Starting our frog adventure with observation activities would heighten children's interest in frogs and give me time to put together cohesive learning experiences for further study.

Safety First

The children were more excited than I'd ever seen them. Immediately, they wanted to put their hands into the pond and grab the eggs. My first job was to teach them how to study animals safely. Back in the classroom, we reviewed germs and how they are transmitted. I showed children pictures of what "germs" look like under a microscope and introduced the term *bacteria*. After explaining that germs are invisible, we pretended tiny pieces of paper were bacteria. To help the children understand how bacteria travel, we scattered the pieces of paper all over the classroom. Our strategy to prevent bacteria from spreading to us or from us to the frogs was to wash our hands before and after our observation studies.

Second, I did not want the children to harm the eggs, tadpoles, or frogs in any way during our study. We discussed how to treat animals carefully and how to be gentle with animals, so they would not be squished or dropped. I told students that the classroom aide and I would be the only people to scoop up eggs and tadpoles so the eggs would not get hurt.

Third, I had to ensure the children's safety working around standing water. Normally the pond is covered unless the class is working there, and now I couldn't cover it. Because West Nile virus is a concern in our area, I decided to check the pond every morning for mosquito larvae and to scoop it out in advance before any student visited the pond—however, during the study no mosquito larvae materialized.

The children and I created pond rules to keep ourselves safe. This is what the children came up with:

- Work at the pond only when an adult is with you.
- Wear protective clothing, such as aprons, to stay dry.
- Kneel down when looking in the pond.
- No drinking pond water.
- No running around the pond.
- Do not splash in the pond water.
- Do not touch eggs or other creatures in the pond.

Many of these rules had already been established in the context of the water center. However, with the new name *pond* I wanted to make sure students would follow water safety rules no matter what the context.

Frogspawn Hatch Quickly

To study our frogs, I decided to start each day with an observation period of about 30 minutes. During this time we would focus on making observations and discuss what we saw. Our first observation day was wonderful. The children wore aprons and crowded around the pool on their knees. Their eyes were drawn to the blobs of jelly floating around in the water. We taped a large piece of chart paper to the wall of the preschool on which to record our observations. Using markers, the children took turns helping to draw a large picture of the pond.

The children gathered in a circle on our vinyl outside floor, and I scooped up a clump of eggs using a small bucket. The bucket was passed around the circle, and we discussed the eggs' color, size, number, and what we thought might hatch. Students estimated there were about 100 eggs. One child noticed that not all of the eggs looked the same. Sure enough, some blobs were more clear and seemed to be squiggly. After each child looked at the eggs in the bucket, they went to the chart paper and drew frogspawn on our pond picture.

The next day, the children were even more excited about the pond. What seemed like hundreds of tiny tadpoles were now squiggling around in the water, including some still in jelly blobs. We repeated the procedure of the day before, writing our observations, passing around a small sample in the bucket, and drawing tadpoles on the chart paper. When all the children began asking, "What will they eat?," I knew we'd have to begin our frog research right away.

Asking and Answering Questions

Back in the classroom, we discussed what we knew about ponds, tadpoles, and frogs. Basically, students knew that ponds were outside, had fish and frogs in them, and were muddy. Tadpoles were cute, and frogs were green, ate bugs, and could jump and say "ribbit" or "croak." During this discussion, I had each child think of a question about frogs that they wanted to answer. The range of their questions ensured that we would cover a variety of topics. Here are a few examples.

- "What kind of frogs are they?"
- "How do they jump? How will we find them if they jump away?"
- "Are tadpoles fish?"
- "Why do they change?"
- "What do they eat?"

I decided to focus on "Are tadpoles fish?" and "Why do they change?" first. After all, the tadpoles were changing rapidly and the life cycle is a fascinating topic. After our observation time each day, I read books about fish and amphibians to the children.

We looked for anything in the books that matched what we were seeing in the pond. We made a chart listing the differences so the children could see why the frogs were amphibians and to understand what an amphibian is.

Typically, story time was followed by a hands-on activity. For example, students made clay models of each stage of the frog's life cycle, and we learned or created songs about frogs and their changes. Students' favorite activity was to pantomime the life cycle of a frog.

From Tadpole to Frog

As the tadpoles grew larger, I supplied each child with a 8-oz. clear plastic cup in which students could observe a tadpole up close. Because the children had been extremely careful and respectful of the rules thus far—and it was taking too much time for me to catch a tadpole for each child with our aquarium net—I decided to let the children try to carefully scoop up a tadpole using their plastic cups. They scooped in groups of three students at three different points of the pond. Students who became careless—standing up, throwing water, or trying to grab with their hands—were not allowed to continue.

I soon discovered that children were more adept than me at collecting tadpoles.

The plastic cups had a magnifying effect, so students could really see the details on the tadpoles. As the tadpoles swam around in the water in the cups, the children were amazed at how quickly the tadpoles were changing. Within a week, some tadpoles had back legs.

After the observation period, students returned the frogs to the pond. Each observation period the children were wondering if they were scooping up the same tadpole as the day before. As the adult frogs appeared, we added some fireplace-sized logs for them to sit on. The frogs were tiny, ranging from marble to superball size.

To get a frog in their cups, students would hold the cup close and lightly tap the frog from behind. The frog almost always jumped right into the cup. It was very difficult to keep the adult frogs in the cup. Many times they would jump out and away into the grass. I did not allow the children to chase them for fear that the frogs would be stepped on and killed.

I asked the children to document the changing tadpoles every day by drawing what was in their cups. They dictated a sentence to be written with each change. Within a month, each child had created a book about the change from tadpole to frog.

What Kind of Frog?

Meanwhile, I filled our classroom with many posters and books about the life cycle of a frog, and I incorporated frogs into our curriculum in any way I could. For mathematics explorations, we graphed how long it took for the frogs to change in our pond. (It took a total of three months for all of the tadpoles to change. We wondered why some tadpoles took a week and others months. The children thought the faster-changing tadpoles were stronger or were eating all the food in the pond.) We estimated how many frogs we had in each stage of development. The first week we felt we had about 50 tadpoles in the pond. The second week we had about 10 with front or back legs. By the third week we estimated 30 of them had front or back legs and maybe 10 that were still just a tail. By the fourth week we estimated we had 10 frogs. We never had more than 10 frogs at any one time, because they would leave the pond soon after becoming adults.

The frogs were small—approximately 2 cm compared with 4–5 cm as tadpoles, smooth, and light green in color. The children observed that the frogs had three sticky toes on each foot, which were "tickly." Because algae was growing in the pond and various tiny water bugs were swimming around, we guessed that was what the tadpoles and little frogs ate. Based on information from our resource books, we decided that we had a type of tree frog.

Learning Opportunities

During our frog days of summer, we also took field trips to local ponds to see if what was happening in our pond was also occurring in real ponds. I introduced students to the concept of the pond as a habitat, and students and I started looking for other aspects of pond life. Our pond now had a great algae community, several types of aquatic insects, and a lily pad I purchased at a garden center. I also prepared slides with our pond water to look for microscopic animals in the water using our video-screen microscope. The learning experiences seemed as if they would never end.

To check my students' progress, I developed several activities to see if they understood the life cycle and characteristics of amphibians. First, I made cards showing the different stages of a frog's life cycle. The children were tested individually by having them arrange the cards in the correct order. All of the four- and five-year-olds could do this easily. Of my five three-year-olds, only two could put the cards in the right order consistently.

Second, I presented the students with picture cards of different body parts of many amphibians, fish, mammals, and insects. The children were asked to build a frog and to put their frog into one of four habitat backgrounds—sky, ocean, pond scene, and forest. All of the children could do this consistently.

I also evaluated the pictures and models the students made for accuracy and details. During our many discussions I could tell which students were retaining information and which were forgetting information previously presented.

Leaving the Pond

As the frogs matured and left the pond, the children's distress grew at losing them. By the third month, it was increasingly obvious that soon there would be no frogs left in the pond. The children begged to keep some of the frogs. I decided that to continue exploring the idea of habitat, we would construct an indoor terrarium for a few of our frogs.

I found an old 20-gal. aquarium and set it up next to an aquarium already in the

> **Connecting to the Standards**
> This article relates to the following *National Science Education Standards* (NRC 1996):
>
> **Content Standards**
> **Grades K–4**
>
> **Standard A: Science as Inquiry**
> * Abilities necessary to do scientific inquiry
>
> **Standard C: Life Science**
> * Characteristics of organisms
> * Life cycles of organisms
> * Organisms and environments

classroom. We filled the terrarium using dirt, rocks, and moss from our school yard. A layer of dirt was put in and rocks, moss, and a small branch were arranged on top. A shallow pool was created in the center by putting a small bowl in the dirt layer. We filled the bowl with water from the pond.

Finally, it was time to put in our frogs. I decided five frogs would be appropriate for the space we had, and the students and I transferred them indoors. The children were ecstatic. The frogs did very well for two weeks. However, for some reason, one by one, the frogs would go into the water and drown. Within a month, we lost all five of our frogs.

We tried to prevent the frogs from drowning, but decreasing the water did not help, and local pet stores that carried frogs did not offer us any advice, nor could I find information about our problem on the internet or in the books I had. The students were sad but did not seem too upset.

We added a discussion of death to our life cycle. We shared stories of any pets anyone had lost before. They told me how they felt sad and missed their old pet. We talked about accidents and old age deaths. We decided the frogs had accidental deaths because they had kept going in the water in their terrarium and drowning. As a group, we decided the frogs were better off left outside so they could live a normal frog life. The children were happy at the thought that, if they looked carefully enough, they could still get to see frogs outside.

In retrospect, I would not attempt the indoor terrarium again. However, we are planning to create a permanent pond on our school property so we can study frogs and their habitat all year long and, with much scrubbing, regain our water center on the playground.

Audrey L. Coffey (mactk@comcast.net) *is the director of Discovery Preschool Learning Center in Manassas, Virginia. Donna R. Sterling is associate professor of science education and director of the Center for Restructuring Education in Science and Technology at George Mason University in Fairfax, Virginia.*

Resources

Kwan, T., and J. Texley. 2002. *Exploring safely: A guide for elementary teachers.* Arlington, VA: NSTA Press.

National Research Council (NRC). 1996. *National Science Education Standards.* Washington, DC: National Academy Press.

Science Centers for All

Classroom science centers allow children to collaborate and be instrumental in their science learning.

Leslie Irwin, Christine Nucci, and E. Carol Beckett

With diversity in classrooms across the nation increasing every year, teachers are more challenged than ever to equitably engage all students in high quality science activities. No longer is it unusual for elementary teachers to have students from different cultural, socioeconomic, physiological, and linguistic backgrounds in the same classroom.

Children's differences can present unique needs that may require adjustments of teaching environments and styles. But how can a teacher meet these special needs and still provide quality learning for all? We suggest it can be done by fostering cultural awareness and sensitivity among students through the use of science centers in the classroom.

As professors of education at Arizona State University West in Phoenix, we have seen the success of science centers through our work with children and preservice teachers and would like to share our experiences.

Celebrating Students' Differences

Science learning can be made more effective when teachers acknowledge and appreciate students' differences—whether they are gender, ethnic, exceptional, or other—and tailor classroom learning to embrace the differences. And science learning centers—designated areas in the classroom where students explore materials or objects and conduct open-ended science activities in a nonthreatening way—can be an excellent tool for teachers to encourage positive interaction among students of different backgrounds and ability levels.

At science centers, students can begin to develop understanding of topics from their own cultural perspective at their own pace. Typically, activities conducted at classroom science centers are open-ended in nature and address the current topics of study. Many times the activities focus on enrichment or concept review.

Teachers can drive the planning and creation of science centers that celebrate the diversity of the students in their classroom. Some ideas:

- Find books, resources, or information cards that identify positive contributions of individuals from the people of the same cultural backgrounds as the students in your class and create a science center that identifies them.
- Offer opportunities for children to investigate something from their backgrounds. For example, in a geology science center include samples of rocks indigenous to countries from which students come.
- Have students bring in cultural objects from home to investigate at a science center.
- In these ways, students and teachers can learn about each other as they share their discoveries.

Working Together to Learn More

Depending on its purpose, a science center can involve either independent or group work. Group work at science centers particularly helps English language learners and students for whom language skills do not come easily.

For example, teachers might have a group of students with different backgrounds and ability levels work together to develop hypotheses and agree on those to pursue for experimentation. By working together at a science center, everyone in the group is a participant in the project and feels ownership of the assignment.

Group work can also facilitate acquisition of both social and academic listening, speaking, reading, and writing skills, which can help to build students' self-esteem. Often students' self-esteem rises as their language skills increase, making them feel more a part

of the class. Additionally, English language learners benefit by learning names and vocabulary associated with the objects found in the science centers through the manipulations and modifications of these materials (Kessler and Quinn 1987).

Access for All

The space allocated for a science center is another important factor in its success. An effective science center is accessible to *all* students—including exceptional students, those needing better interpersonal skills, English language learners, and others. There should be ample space for students to maneuver around, the materials should be available and within easy reach, and the center should not be disruptive to the classroom flow.

We've found it effective to set up a science center in a corner of the classroom or along the classroom's center wall space. There we've placed tables with three-sided cardboard dividers for displays—changed according to the topics of study—and room for two or three chairs. This setup allows the teacher maximum flexibility—some children can be working at the science center while others are involved in teacher-directed learning in the rest of the room.

Times for students to work at the science center can be scheduled in various ways—during regular science instruction; during individual time (when other tasks are completed, such as a free-time choice); or, if a teacher is available to supervise, prior to and/or after the scheduled school day. The key is making sure all of the students have an opportunity to explore the materials at the center at one time or another.

Diversity in Materials

Careful selection of culturally or age-appropriate activities and materials is also vital in providing meaningful experiences for students at science centers. To ensure that the center reflects the diversity of students in your classroom, provide a wide variety of materials from children's surroundings, including some familiar and unfamiliar cultural objects or artifacts. One suggestion might be to ask students to bring in some interesting objects from their own homes to investigate at a science center. Such an activity would give all students an opportunity to share something important from their own backgrounds.

Some common science center materials might include bamboo and gourds for creating sound; empty cans and strings for making string telephones; and paper, sticks, glue, rubber bands, paper towel tubes, and bottle caps to create items such as kites, periscopes, or pinhole cameras that demonstrate scientific concepts.

Provide materials that children can manipulate in any manner without concern for destruction or cost of replacement and that can be modified with any possible imagination. These experiences with household items turned into "experimental" objects may be the ones that help students learn basic science approaches.

Simplicity in Directions

Another element that is important to the success of a science center is clarity in instruction. Be sure that the center includes clear directions for the activity and rules of conduct at the center. Providing activity sheets with icons illustrating the scientific terms or the steps of the activity are helpful to children who are not fully fluent in English.

Tape recorders and tapes containing information about the center topic will provide auditory lesson review for English language learners, sharpening their listening comprehension at the same time.

Finally, providing a selection of books with both illustrations and text allows all students to expand their field of information gathering.

Benefits for All

Children are captivated by scientific investigations and describe what they observe in language characteristic of their backgrounds, experience, and levels of development. These include reactions of disbelief, invitations to other students to come see what is happening, taking ownership for results, calling the teacher's attention to something "weird" happening, and wanting to do the activity over and over for the sheer joy of it.

It is through these types of activities that children develop such skills of scientific inquiry as classification, comparison, communication, inference, prediction, measurement, use of numbers, space/time relations, conclusions, and observation, thereby discovering the natural scientist within them. Through such learning processes, children are able to formulate knowledge, attitudes, behaviors, and views of the world in which they live.

Classroom science centers allow children to collaborate and be instrumental in their science learning—an ongoing process they create to investigate and understand their environments. By encouraging and providing equal opportunities for all students regardless of ethnicity, gender, language, class, and exceptionalities, a teacher can make the pursuit of science a motivating and exciting experience for all involved. In these situations a sense of acceptance, belonging, and cooperation exists among the students. Ultimately, the sharing and cooperation among students at science centers culminates in the learning of science.

Leslie Irwin is an associate professor of elementary education, Christine Nucci is an assistant professor of childhood education, and E. Carol Beckett is an assistant professor of English as a Second Language Education, all in the College of Education at Arizona State University West, in Phoenix, Arizona.

Resources

Barba, R. H. 1995. *Science in a multicultural classroom. A guide to teaching and learning.* Boston: Allyn and Bacon.

Kessler, C., and M. E. Quinn. 1987. ESL and science learning. In ed. J. Crandall, *ESL through content-area instruction: Mathematics, science, social studies,* 55–87. Englewood Cliffs, NJ.: Prentice Hall.

Rillero, P., and J. Allison, eds. 1997. *Creative childhood experiences in mathematics and science: Projects, activity series, and centers for early childhood.* Columbus, OH: ERIC Clearinghouse for Science, Mathematics, and Environmental Education.

Project Reptile!

When kindergarten students explore a topic of their own choosing, the result is good science learning.

Deborah Diffily

Good teachers continually plan learning experiences to help young children make connections within and among areas of study (Zemelman et al. 1998). Integrating curriculum is important in helping children make these connections. Class projects offer an effective child-centered approach that helps organize and integrate curriculum. Class projects differ from other methods of integrating curriculum in that projects are

* studies of children-selected topics,
* research based,
* directed by children with guidance from the teacher,
* conducted over a period of weeks, and
* concluded with the children sharing what they learned.

One successful class project, conducted by a group of my kindergarten students—building a reptile exhibit—came out of the students' great interest in reptiles.

The school where I taught is a public school with a mission of challenging tradi-tional assumptions of education. Applied-learning projects were encouraged there, and individual teachers facilitated child-directed projects. By definition, students involved in an applied-learning project must share what they learned with a spe-cific audience. The reptile exhibit project motivated students to learn above grade-level expectations and addressed standards identified by the National Science Educa-tion Standards (NRC 1996). In planning and implementing the reptile exhibit, I ad-dressed Teaching Standards A, B, C, D, and E, and students met Content Standards A, C, E, and G (see Standards box).

Throughout the eight weeks of plan-ning, working on different components of the exhibit, and giving tours, the children continued their typical daily schedule mi-nus a few minutes from each activity. The time taken from the other routines totaled almost one hour, so the last hour of the day was dedicated to project time. See "Timeline for Reptiles Exhibit Project" for more details about what the class did each week.

How It All Started

The kindergarten students already knew quite a bit about reptiles. They had observed and cared for classroom pets—a rat snake and two box turtles—for several months. The classroom's science center was full of books about reptiles and the children returned to these books week after week. What really set the project in motion, however, was a student's birthday party held at the local zoo. Everyone in the class had been invited and talk of the party filled the class for days before and after the event. The herpetarium was the children's favorite exhibit. Conversations about the reptiles dominated the classroom. During a class meeting the week after the party, two students persuaded their classmates that they needed to know "more, much more" about reptiles.

Research, Research, Research

Learning about reptiles involved many activities over the next several days, and students' knowledge and skills were enhanced in various content areas. For example, students compared the eating habits of our class' box turtles. Every afternoon they fed the two turtles the same type and amount of food. They then drew pictures of the food, and each day they marked off with an *X* the food that had been eaten. By testing different foods listed in a book on turtles' diets, students tried to determine which foods our turtles preferred. They also tested situations that make turtles retreat into their shells.

Topic: Reptiles
at *www.scilinks.org*
Enter code: SC0401

Conducting research strengthened the children's literacy development in multiple ways. Students listened to books read aloud and responded to them by drawing pictures. They learned to read sight words, such as *turtle, tortoise, snake, lizard, alligator,* and *crocodile,* from the labels in the science center where they sorted and posted photographs of reptiles. Older students often read parts of books to the kindergartners to help them understand the pictures.

During their research, students collected reptile facts for about two weeks. Students dictated facts they had learned and identified whether they learned the information from a book or from observation. The students sorted the facts by source. Then, using published animal fact cards as models, the children rewrote the fact in their best handwriting and sketched reptiles to create their own fact cards. Some students compiled the fact cards into their own reptile books.

Several students wrote letters to administrators and families to coordinate field trips to view reptile exhibits. Others wrote letters to personnel at a science museum and at the zoo to schedule class visits. The students wrote all of the letters themselves, using the level of developmental spelling that they were capable of doing. I included a transcription of the letter, so the adult receiving it did not have to struggle to read it.

Students learned to seek help from topic experts through my prompting through questions such as "Can you think of anyone we met on our field trips who might know a lot about lizards?" Students also e-mailed questions to reptile experts in several cities. One student, Drew, for example, had a sister who was taking a biology class at

Figure 1. Students made reptile fact cards to share their growing knowledge.

"Gila monsters shed skin."

"Snakes are long"

an Austin college. When Drew wondered why horned toads squirt blood from their eyes, we could not find the answer in any book. Drew wanted his sister to help. She explained the situation to her professor, and he agreed to accept e-mails from Drew. Drew posed the questions: "Wut do raptils eeyt? How dus a horn tod spit blud owt of his eye?" I also contacted the professor before Drew wrote.

Building the Reptile Exhibit

After field trips to a local science and history museum, students decided that they wanted to create their own exhibit on reptiles. Convinced that they knew more about reptiles than any other class in the school and confident that they could do just about anything,

the children decided that they could create this exhibit in "just a few days."

Applied learning projects require students to make decisions about project work; however, kindergarten students have few experiences that prepare them for this. I used a pondering approach to lead the students to consider suggestions: "I was thinking last night that we are learning a lot about reptiles. I wonder if we could make an exhibit like they have at the zoo." If the students did not accept the suggestion, then I let it drop. After making leading suggestions, I followed and supported the students' decisions regarding planning the exhibit.

The first planning step was to hold a class meeting and brainstorm ideas. We decided to include in the exhibit pictures they

Timeline for Reptiles Exhibit Project

Week 1:

- Vote to study reptiles.
- As a class, read books about reptiles.
- Start listing possible resources.
- Begin collecting documentation about what is learned and storing it in pocket folders.
- Write facts.
- Draw pictures of reptiles.
- Write letters to experts.

Week 2:

- As a class, begin reading downloaded information from internet sites.
- Continue writing facts about reptiles and drawing pictures.
- Write more letters to experts.
- Mark pages of books and articles to be photocopied for project folders.

Week 3:

- Plan field trips to see reptiles at the zoo and museum.
- Continue writing facts about reptiles and marking pages of books and articles to be photocopied for project folders.
- Create reptile pictures in different media.
- Write reptile stories, books, and poems.

Week 4:

- Take field trips to zoo and science museum.
- Do group research.

Week 5:

- Measure the room to be used for the exhibit.
- Make floor plans and arrange furniture.
- Discuss and make lists of what should be included in the exhibit.
- Decide how items in the exhibit should be displayed.

Week 6:

- Write letters to borrow reptile specimens from the science museum.
- Create more pictures of reptiles using various media.
- Hang these pictures for the entrance to the exhibit.
- Create and send out invitations to exhibit opening.
- Create and distribute a memo inviting classes in school to tour the exhibit.
- Discuss criteria for a good brochure.
- Draft exhibit brochure copy.
- Finalize and make copies of the brochure.

Week 7:

- Finish hanging facts and pictures.
- Set up specimens with labels.
- Hold museum opening for families and special friends of the class.

Week 8:

- Give tours to other classes and visitors to the school.

had drawn, books they had made, books we had read, and our class snake and turtles.

The students had seen a photograph essay at the museum, so they decided to make their own photograph display as part of their exhibit. Several children had taken photographs of the animals on the field trip using the class camera. Students chose photographs from the field trip and wrote labels to describe each photograph. The students used the writing process to write the label copy. They drafted, edited, and revised their labels. I helped them stretch out the words verbally so they could more easily hear the sounds in those words. I did not spell for them, nor did I type their labels.

Once students had decided on the words to include on the picture label, they conferred with their classmates to make sure the copy explained the photograph and to ensure that others would understand what they had written. Many of the students could read each other's labels. Because many of the families had become familiar with the children's developmental spelling from examples I had been sending home all year, they were adept at reading the student's efforts.

Then students typed the copy in final form on the class computer and mounted the photograph and label copy onto poster board cut to a standard size. The students used glue sticks to attach the photographs and labels.

It's Almost Showtime

Students worked on the exhibit items for three weeks while continuing their research. As the exhibit date drew nearer, the class asked the custodian to bring tables to the basement so they could set up the exhibit. Students placed a few items on the tables:

- the turtles and snake from the class's science center
- books children had written about different reptiles

On the floor they taped lizard, turtle, and alligator footprints to indicate which way visitors should walk through the exhibit.

The students and I met in the basement to evaluate their efforts. The children approved the walls and the floor, but they decided they needed more live reptiles to put on the tables—two live specimens were not enough for the exhibit. With my help, students successfully e-mailed a museum staff member and asked to borrow specimens from the museum's teaching collection.

Students also chose other items to hang on the museum walls including:
- their original reptile drawings and paintings
- labeled photographs from nature magazines and field trips
- the fact cards

The children displayed different orders of reptiles on different-colored poster board (snakes and lizards—blue; turtles and tortoises—red; alligators and crocodiles—green). The fact cards were glued on the same color posterboard as the specimens.

At this point the children worked in groups finishing last-minute details. We kept running lists of things to do for the exhibit opening. The groups formed as students volunteered to do things. I did not assign students to work together. If there was a task no one volunteered for, I might ask one or two students to volunteer.

In one group the children examined brochures they had collected at the museum. Students discussed the criteria for good brochures and created their own exhibit brochure guided by their list of characteristics. According to their criteria, a good brochure

- has lots of words,
- tells what is in the exhibit,
- has pictures with lots of details, and
- is folded.

Another group of students made promotional signs and posters about the exhibit.

The class designed a museum opening invitation for parents, grandparents, friends, and volunteers. With help from older students they looked up addresses in the telephone book and in the school directory and addressed their own envelopes. Some students worked on a note to all the teachers in the school inviting all classes to schedule a tour of the exhibit. They kept track of the tours on our large class calendar after I modeled for them how I keep track of my meetings.

Exhibit Day

On the day of the exhibit opening, more than 60 adults crowded into the museum exhibit space. The opening was two hours long and was invitation only for family and friends of the class. The tour wasn't scripted, and the excitement of the kindergarten students was evident as they acted as docents for those who came to the opening. The rest of the week was spent giving tours to other students in the school and visitors to the building.

Project Lessons

Through this project students learned important lessons they might not have learned in more traditional science-related instruction (Manning et al. 1994). Students learned

that they could find fascinating facts about reptiles through multiple resources. For example, students dictated to me that they had learned

- A turtle is a reptile.
- A snake is a reptile.
- Reptiles shed their skin.
- Some snakes eat eggs.
- Our snake eats dead mice.
- Snakes don't chew.

Some higher-ability students, who were particularly engaged in finding unusual facts, dictated such facts:

- King snakes eat other snakes.
- Horned toads squirt blood from their eyes.
- Frilled lizards puff up their frills to scare enemies.

The students learned that they could record these facts and read them to other people. They learned that they could write letters and have adults write back to them. They learned about working as a team member and finding solutions while making group decisions. And through the reactions of the visitors to their museum exhibit, they learned that they could create important products that adults took seriously. Through their involvement in researching reptiles and creating a museum exhibit that people came to tour, students learned that they could do important work.

In any given project, the topic will vary and the specific topic will drive the type of research that is conducted (Wolk 1998). Based on their knowledge and skills, different groups of children will determine various ways to organize the information they discover. Not every group of children will choose a museum exhibit to demonstrate what they have learned. They may decide to create a brochure, write a book, or produce an informational video.

Virtually any science topic can become the focus for a class project. Any group of elementary students can learn to come to consensus about a topic to study, conduct research, make day-to-day decisions about locating resources, organize what is being learned, and select a way of sharing with others what they have learned. Any group can genuinely learn through science projects.

Deborah Diffily is an assistant professor in the Department of Early Childhood Education at Southern Methodist University in Dallas, Texas.

Resources

American Association for the Advancement of Science. 1993. *Benchmarks for science literacy.* New York: Oxford University.

Dewey, J. 1938. *Experience and education.* New York: Collier.

Edwards, C., L. Gandini, and G. Forman. 1998. *The hundred languages of children: The Reggio Emilia approach—advanced reflections.* Greenwich, CT: Ablex.

Katz, L., and S. Chard. 2000. *Engaging children's minds: The project approach.* 2nd ed. Norwood, NJ: Ablex.

Kilpatrick, W. H. 1918. The project method. *Teachers College Record* 19 (4): 319–325.

Manning, M., G. Manning, and R. Long. 1994. *Theme immersion: Inquiry-based curriculum in elementary and middle schools.* Portsmouth, NH: Heinemann.

National Research Council (NRC). 1996. *National Science Education Standards.* Washington, DC: National Academy Press.

Tanner, L. N. 1990. *Dewey's laboratory school: Lessons for today.* New York: Teachers College.

Wolk, S. 1998. *A democratic classroom.* Portsmouth, NH: Heinemann.

Zemelman, S., H. Daniels, and A. A. Hyde. 1998. *Best practice: New standards for teaching and learning in America's schools.* 2nd ed. Portsmouth, NH: Heinemann.

Connecting to the Standards

This article relates the following National Science Education Standards (NRC 1996):

Teaching Standard A:

Teachers of science plan an inquiry-based science program for their students.

Teaching Standard B:

Teachers of science guide and facilitate learning.

Teaching Standard C:

Teachers of science engage in ongoing assessment of their teaching and of student learning.

Teaching Standard D:

Teachers of science design and manage learning environments that provide students with the time, space, and resources needed for learning science.

Teaching Standard E:

Teachers of science develop communities of science learners that reflect the intellectual rigor of scientific inquiry and the attitudes and social values conducive to science learning.

Content Standard A:

As a result of activities in grades K–4, all students should develop understanding of:

- abilities necessary to do scientific inquiry
- understanding about scientific inquiry

Content Standard C:

As a result of activities in grades K–4, all students should develop understanding of:

- the characteristics of organisms
- life cycles of organisms
- organisms and environments

Content Standard E:

As a result of activities in grades K–4, all students should develop
- abilities of technological design
- understanding of science and technology
- abilities to distinguish between natural objects and objects made by humans

Content Standard G:

As a result of activities in grades K–4, all students should develop understanding of science as a human endeavor.

A Science Night of Fun

A university community helps students and parents experience interactive science learning in a new way.

Katie Rommel-Esham and Andrea Castellitto

Every spring, K–5 students from a local elementary school look forward to participating in Science Night. Science Night is an opportunity for members of our educational community to come together and enjoy science learning from a new perspective—one that takes science outside the classroom walls. Sponsored by State University of New York College (SUNY) at Geneseo in Geneseo, New York, this project brings together elementary students, parents, and university students and faculty for an evening of fun, meaningful science experiments, demonstrations, and activities.

Because science learning is often confined to a classroom, Science Night presents science experiences in a new setting with the purpose of making science accessible and enjoyable to everyone. Our university's Science Night program could easily serve as a model for any school interested in generating enthusiasm for science among teachers, students, and parents.

Science Night has its roots in "Family Math," a program our university's school of education implements each fall in conjunction with a local elementary school. Since the response to Family Math night was so great, we decided to host a similar evening with a focus on science. We hoped Science Night would give students and their parents an opportunity to interact with science topics in a new way. Our goal was to show participants that they can interact, learn something new, and incorporate science into everyday situations.

Project Planning

As with any large project, the first step involved detailed planning. About two months before the event, I selected an undergraduate student to coordinate the event and start planning—choosing activities, creating materials lists, and getting documents ready to be photocopied. From my perspective as event organizer, having a preservice teacher as coordinator was a lifesaver. She helped perform many of the tasks, like photocopying and e-mailing the other teacher candidates who were involved. She also determined which activities were appropriate for the event and which should go home with the students. This was mostly a question of logistics—we can't plant a garden in the cafeteria, for example.

Next, interested parties—the undergraduate coordinator, a college faculty member, a parent council representative from the participating school, and a fourth-grade teacher—met over a two-week period and selected the activities. We planned on having about six weeks from initial planning to the night of the event, so things wouldn't be rushed. A total of 11 activities were chosen from various sources (see "Resources").

The planning group tried to include a variety of lessons and topics so that everyone involved connected on some level to at least one activity. The group used the national and state learning standards, district curriculum, and the interests of students as a guide for choosing the activities. These guidelines helped the group relate the activities to students' science classroom content.

We began recruiting college volunteers about a month ahead of time. We found that it was unnecessary to offer students in methodology courses incentives such as extra credit to participate in such events. Once the word was out, the students reminded us that they wanted to help.

After the activities were chosen, the preservice teachers worked in pairs to prepare the lessons. They worked over a two-week period making posters advertising their activities, researching any background information related to their activities, and preparing to implement the activities—essentially doing a dry run to make sure everything worked as they thought it would. Methods instructors provided the preservice teachers with copies of their activity sheets and other resources so they could familiarize themselves with the activity and its related scientific principles. The school of education, the elementary parent council, and the school district provided additional support.

Getting the Word Out

The parent council, a cosponsor of the event, was responsible for advertising, collecting "intent to attend" sheets, providing refreshments, securing the room, and making the appropriate arrangements with the school district. They also helped with setting up before and cleaning up after the event and provided funding for any materials that were needed.

Elementary teachers were also involved in the advertisement at the classroom level—providing students with general information about the event, giving students assignments of things to look for as they participated, or offering a homework bonus coupon for attendance.

Teachers wanted to recruit upper elementary (grades 3–5) students. Often, parents of younger students are willing to come to family learning events, but not the parents of older students. Sparking these students' interest in attending worked well for the intermediate- aged group.

The Event

When Science Night arrived, the teacher candidates set up the room and distributed the necessary materials. The school cafeteria tables were arranged into a semicircular formation to allow students and their families to move easily around the room and to make sure there was plenty of space for a small group to participate in each activity. Along

Take-Home Activities

How Do You Make an Egg Float?
An exploration of how adding salt to water affects density.

Two Water Towers
An exploration of how water tower size affects flow rate.

Trick Straw Race
An investigation of the effect of placing pinpoint holes in a drinking straw.

Science Night Activities

All Grades:
The Rainstick—Students make rainsticks using paper towel tubes and nails and experiment to see how different filler materials (unpopped popcorn kernels, rice, beans, split peas) produce different sounds.

Kazoo—Students use toilet paper tubes and waxed paper to create kazoos.

Secret Message—Students create messages with lemon juice and milk.

Kindergarten:
Bean Sprouts—Students examine lima beans from sprouting bean to growing plant.

Rubbings—What details can be enhanced by creating crayon rubbings of natural objects?

First grade:
Full Cup—How does surface tension affect the number of paper clips you can drop into a full glass of water?

Goo—Students investigate the properties of liquids and solids using cornstarch and water.

Popping Ping-Pong Balls—How many pennies do you need to make a ping-pong ball sink?

Second grade:
Hearing Things—Sound changes as it travels from spoons hitting a table through a string to our ears.

Spinning Colors—Can black and white really make colors?

Third grade:
Skin Prints—What kind of fingerprints do you have?

Tasting Center—Students examine where different kinds of taste buds are located.

Fourth grade:
Faking Fossils—Students "create" fossils with natural materials and plaster of paris.

An Oily Mess—Students investigate the effect of an "oil spill" on the environment.

Fifth grade:
Copter—Using paper and paper clips, students investigate aerodynamics and what factors affect the flight of their "helicopter."

Which Drops Faster?—Does an object's mass affect how quickly it will fall?

with the activity tables, there were also a sign-in table and an estimation table.

At the back of the cafeteria, a refreshment table was set up with fruit, cookies, and juice for the participants to enjoy as the evening progressed. As a souvenir of the evening, "science wizard" stickers and bookmarks were also distributed.

As the students arrived and signed in, they received manila folders—prepared by the undergraduate event coordinator and another preservice teacher candidate—with directions for each of the evening's science activities as well as directions for a few activities to try on their own at home (see "Take-Home Activities"). Students could refer to these folders as they made their way through the activities.

Students signed in by using a dichotomous key to find their place in the chart. This helped—whether students knew it or not—to reinforce the ideas of categorization and well-defined sets. At the estimation table, primary-aged students guessed the number of miniature candy bars and intermediate-level students guessed the number of chocolate kisses. These required minimal preparation and setup, yet served to reinforce an important concept for all of the students. In all cases, the estimates were written on Post-it notes and used to create a bar graph. The winners—who took home the goody jars—were revealed toward the end of the evening.

Once inside, participants began their journey into various science activities and projects. Students and their families investigated the properties of "goo," made parachutes, made energy shift from potential to kinetic, tested the effect of gravity on falling objects, cre-

ated rainsticks, explored their taste buds, examined sprouting lima beans at various stages, played with Cartesian divers, examined their fingerprints, and conducted many other activities (see "Science Night Activities," p. 67). The wide range of science experiences engaged both children and parents.

Parents responded positively to the activities and were involved on all levels. Our idea for this event was that parents not simply act as observers but actually participate along with their children. We wanted them to leave with the understanding that they can support their children in science learning at home with readily found materials.

To that end, the preservice teacher candidates who led the activities were instructed to facilitate the interactions between the elementary students and their parents and not be the ones who guided them through the activities—that was the role of their parents.

Parents responded well to this and seemed glad to have the opportunity to interact with their children in this way. All evening, mothers and fathers stood on chairs and dropped things, played with the goo, and made rainsticks alongside their children— they learned and had fun!

Positive Reinforcement

Participation in Science Night provided a variety of positive experiences for all involved. The teacher candidates were able to work with students in an informal setting that was comfortable and relaxed. Planning the event also enabled them to examine their own understanding of the science concepts presented throughout the night.

For many of the teacher candidates, the success of Science Night reinforced their decision to become teachers. Many teachers discovered that Science Night provided an intrinsic reward in much the same way that classroom teaching does.

The students also had a positive experience. They were excited by the enthusiasm the teacher candidates showed for the material they were presenting and did not hesitate to ask questions or challenge information they did not understand. Many were caught up in the idea of working with the older, "cooler" students. Still others seemed excited to be involved in a learning experience with their parents.

Parents Learn Too!

Throughout the event we emphasized the idea that parents can engage in meaningful science experiences with their children.

Because the parents jumped in and explored the science concepts along with their children, we hoped that this would help develop camaraderie and spark an interest in science that would be carried outside the walls of the school building. Indeed, many parents commented that they had forgotten how much fun science learning could be and how easily it could be done as a family.

Parents were glad to have an opportunity to interact with their children in a way that was different from simply helping with homework. They felt that Science Night enabled them to actually take part in their children's learning. Several parents commented that they didn't realize that so many things were considered science and said that they would start including children in home activities that support science learning, such as cooking and baking, gardening, and other things that require problem solving.

All in all, Science Night helped the elementary students, preservice teachers, parents, and classroom teachers gain a new perspective of science—they discovered learning science is an active process that is hands-on as well as minds-on and can be accomplished in ways other than traditional textbook learning.

The teacher candidates had the opportunity to try out some of the strategies they had learned in classes, which reinforced the usefulness of a process-oriented approach to teaching and learning. Many participants left Science Night with the realization that science is a vital, dynamic subject.

Katie Rommel-Esham (rommel@geneseo.edu) *is an assistant professor of mathematics and science education in the Ella Cline Shear School of Education at SUNY College at Geneseo in Geneseo, New York. Andrea Castellitto is a sixth-grade inclusion teacher in Somers Central School District in Somers, New York.*

Resources

Bosak, S. V. 1998. *Science is ... A source book of fascinating facts, projects, and activities.* Ontario, Canada: Scholastic Canada.

Churchill, E. R., L. V. Loeschnig, and M. Mandell. 1998. *365 more simple science experiments with everyday materials.* New York: Workman.

Kenda, M., and P. S. Williams. 1992. *Science wizardry for kids.* New York: Scholastic.

National Research Council (NRC). 1996. *National Science Education Standards.* Washington, DC: National Academy Press.

Potter, J. 1995. *Science in seconds for kids.* New York: Scholastic.

Stenmark, J. K., V. Thompson, and R. Cossey. 1986. *Family math.* Berkeley, CA: Lawrence Hall of Science.

Tolman, M. N., and G .R. Hardy. 1999. *Discovering elementary science: Method, content, and problem-solving activities.* Needham Heights, MA: Allyn and Bacon.

Connecting to the Standards

This article relates to the following National Science Education Standards (NRC 1996):

Teaching Standard A:
Teachers of science plan an inquiry-based science program for their students.

Teaching Standard B:
Teachers of science guide and facilitate learning.

Teaching Standard D:
Teachers of science design and manage learning environments that provide students with the time, space, and resources needed for learning science.

Teaching Standard F:
Teachers of science actively participate in the ongoing planning and development of the school science program.

Professional Development Standard A:
Professional development for teachers of science requires learning essential science content through perspectives and methods of inquiry.

Professional Development Standard B:
Professional development for teachers of science requires integrating knowledge of science, learning, pedagogy, and students; it also requires applying that knowledge to science teaching.

Professional Development Standard C:
Professional development for teachers of science requires building understanding and ability for lifelong learning.

Science Education Program Standard B:
The program of study in science for all students should be developmentally appropriate, interesting, and relevant to students' lives; emphasize student understanding through inquiry; and be connected with other school subjects.

Science Education Program Standard C:
The science program should be coordinated with the mathematics program to enhance student use and understanding of mathematics in the study of science and to improve student understanding of mathematics.

Science Education Program Standard D:
The K–12 program must give students access to appropriate and sufficient resources, including quality teachers, time, materials, and equipment, adequate and safe space, and the community.

Science Education Program Standard E:
All students in the K–12 science program must have equitable access to opportunities to achieve the National Science Education Standards.

Science Education Program Standard F:
Schools must work as communities that encourage, support, and sustain teachers as they implement an effective science program.

Integrating Curricula

First Flight

Even young children can do the important work of science in a collaborative community.

Phyllis Whitin

What's the best way for young children to learn about the natural world in depth? An ongoing scientific study! A yearlong involvement with one topic allows time for both planned and spontaneous lessons and opens opportunities to integrate science into other curriculum areas. Yearlong studies also help facilitate "learning subject matter disciplines in the context of inquiry" (NRC 1996).

I chose bird watching as a yearlong project in my kindergarten classroom. By the end of the year, the children developed a heightened awareness and appreciation of the natural world around them, and they learned many important lessons about the nature of science, including such ideas that scientists observe closely and keep records, scientists access resources, and scientists collaborate with one another. The stories that follow illustrate how children learned these lessons and how I learned to adapt my teaching style to their growing knowledge about and interest in birds.

Classroom Bird Station

Before the school year began, I set up a "bird station" in the classroom by placing a seed feeder and a suction-cup hummingbird feeder on one of our classroom windows. Suction-cup feeders for both seed and nectar are available at bird specialty shops and usually cost $15–$30 depending on the style. I used my own funds to purchase the feeders, but other teachers I know have written grants to set up more elaborate bird-feeding stations.

Inside the classroom I placed a table against the window supplied with drawing and writing tools; *Stokes Beginner's Guide to Birds* (Stokes and Stokes 1996); a few picture books; and two clipboards full of blank paper and observation sheets (Doris 1991). I cut out large photographs of birds from calendars and bird magazines and posted them on the wall near the window. I also hung paper models of birds (purchased at a children's hobby shop), including the Carolina chickadee, cardinal, house finch, tufted titmouse, mourning dove, and the ruby-throated hummingbird, from the ceiling.

During the first two weeks of school, several children visited the bird table during our daily free time. It wasn't long until finches and hummingbirds began to frequent the feeders. The children were excited to see a close-up view of these birds, so I suggested that they use the blank paper or the observation sheets on the station table to draw pictures of what they saw and refer to the picture and reference books as guides.

Most of our initial visitors were finches and hummingbirds. One day, however, a cardinal stopped by. Signaling quickly for the children to hold still, I whispered, "Scientists listen, too." Sure enough, the cardinal emitted its characteristic "chip, chip." After it flew away, I asked the children to describe what they saw and heard. They noticed the cardinal's bold red color, shape of the head (crest), triangular beak, and its chipping noise.

They wanted to know more! Several children found the cardinal's picture in some of our reference books, shared this discovery with the class, and asked me to read the accompanying narrative to the pictures in the book. This interest in bird books continued to build for several weeks. In October, the teaching assistant suggested that we establish a daily forum for children to share information from bird books and their drawings. I found this sharing time became more important than I had originally anticipated. By piquing children's curiosity and giving them time to talk, children teach each other and enthusiasm grows (Gallas 1995, Redding et al. 1998, and Whitin and Whitin 1997).

Sharing Time

As the daily forum ritual became established, I witnessed children teaching one another how to use reference guides. *Stokes Beginner's Guide to Birds* proved especially helpful for these young bird-watchers. Each page provides a large photograph, brief text, a range map, and a few symbols to indicate birds' lifestyle habits, such as which ones frequent bird feeders. The book also groups birds by color, and birds with male/female color differentiation appear in two color sections, each with a photo insert and page number as a cross-reference for the mate.

As the students discovered these features, they shared their knowledge with the class. One girl, for example, found and showed her classmates the cardinal's paired pages, as well as those for the wood duck and red-winged blackbird. Other children followed her example—one student even used the range map to display how the house finch "lives on two sides of the country."

Children also began to notice the presence or absence of the bird feeder symbol in the guides and soon could tell me whether a certain bird "ate seeds." They enthusiastically browsed the adult guides, noting both local species and those from far away.

I was surprised by the power of this book-sharing time—bird-watching had now become part of our classroom culture.

Nature Walk

Since the children showed so much interest in birds and their habitats, I decided to organize a walk through the school's nature trail and invited a professor from a local university to join us. Before embarking on the trail, our guest introduced the children to the work of Margaret Morse Nice (1883–1974), an ornithologist and conservationist who observed birds as a young child and who

Figure 1. A Drawing of a Bird's Flight Path.

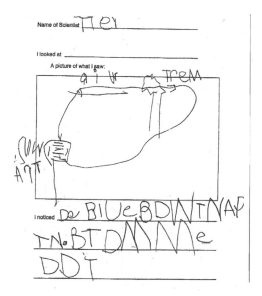

Figure 2. A Bluebird With a Spider in Its Beak.

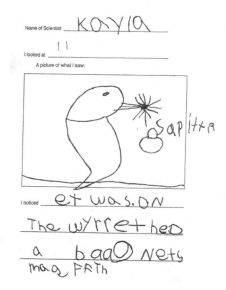

eventually authored six books about birds and their behavior.

The visiting professor explained, "Ms. Nice observed birds closely like you are doing. She wanted to remember what she saw and heard, so she invented codes to show how birds sounded." We asked the children to think about the sound that the cardinal made. "How can we show that sound on paper?" I asked. A few children suggested writing, "T T T" (pronouncing it tih-tih-tih). They also suggested making the letters bigger or smaller to denote volume changes.

Topic: Birds
at *www.scilinks.org*
Enter code: SC0121

The professor and I then showed the children some of Nice's actual codes, which looked like letters or lines slanted up or down to show change in pitch (Ross 1997). Some of her codes included dashes for long notes, dots for short sounds, or imitative words such as "pip."

We also invited the children to draw lines illustrating a bird's flight path. First we asked them to talk about the ways in which they had seen birds fly. Many children responded that they had seen water birds fly at an angle from the water at the beach. Others had seen birds flutter around a bush or feeder. Still others had noticed buzzards that circled over our playground during hot afternoons. Drawing upon these ideas, we asked student volunteers to come to the easel I set up and show how lines could record these different ways to fly. (See Figure 1 for one example of a student's flight path drawing.)

Through these conversations the children understood that they, like Nice, could invent ways to represent sound and flight as well as physical characteristics. They also learned how scientists (in this case, a female who challenged stereotypes of her time) gather the type of information that we read in books.

We couldn't identify too many birds on our walk because they flew away from us. What was important was that we listened to the birds (among them the cardinal and what sounded like crows and bluejays), and hearing birds is a large part of observing them. After listening to a cardinal, many children wrote large strings of "T T T" on their papers. (Each student carried a clipboard and pencil with them on the walk.) Some invented additional symbols, such as "h h a a a" and "D D D." One student explained: "He's saying, 'he, he, he, hi, hi, hi.' Then he stopped saying, 'K hi hi' and said, 'har har har.' They were laughing! That [pointing to the 'D D D'] was a little bird. It was saying, 'Dee Dee Dee.'"

During the walk, the nature professor, teacher assistant, and I also pointed out holes in the trees. "Many of the holes were drilled by woodpeckers," we explained. The children also found smaller holes they thought were made by insects. We stopped to examine a rotting log with fungi growing on it and discussed how trees rot and become part of the soil.

Back in the classroom, the children talked about what they observed during the nature walk, and we assembled their artwork and codes into a class book. During the months that followed, they continued to note and record sounds and flight patterns "like that bird lady did" as one student remarked.

For example, when one boy studied a copy of *Living Bird* (published by Cornell Lab), he found a picture of an ornithologist holding an instrument that looked like a satellite dish. He showed the picture to me and explained that he was sure that the man in the photo was learning about bird sounds. I skimmed the article and agreed: The ornithologist was using the instrument to pick up and record sounds from migrating birds. Happy with his discovery, the child shared with the class how scientists use technology to learn about bird sounds.

Sloppy Eaters?

Throughout the winter months, the children observed more details as they watched birds visit the classroom feeder. For example, while watching house finches in December, two students commented that finches were "sloppy eaters." Building on this cue, we encouraged the children to observe the birds over the next few days to see how the various bird visitors ate, and we discussed their observations at sharing time. Some birds, like the finch, dropped a lot of seeds as they ate. The chickadee usually selected a seed and flew away. The cardinal's strong beak enabled it to crack individual sunflower seeds while discarding the husks.

Shortly after this discussion, titmice began to frequent the feeder. Loud taps attracted the children's attention, and they soon realized that the titmouse, with its more slender beak, held the seed with its feet and pounded it to crack it open. Later in the spring, the hummingbirds returned, and the children noted how this bird used its long, slender beak to gather nectar. When bluebirds arrived, I allowed the children to use binoculars under my supervision so that they could observe these insect-eating birds perching on a nearby wire. (Figure 2 shows one student's observation of a bluebird with a spider in its beak.) As the children made new discoveries, they referred to books for more information on beaks and diets by gathering information from pictures and symbols or by asking adults to read the text aloud.

What a Discovery!

An unexpected bird visited the bird station in January, and the experience showed me just how much the children had learned about how to be a good scientist through their bird-watching. While we were outdoors one afternoon to make our monthly sketch of a tree (another ongoing project), we heard a loud tapping noise—a male sapsucker was drilling on the exact tree we had come to observe! We watched the bird for more than 10 minutes. After it flew away, the children drew what they observed. Most noticed black and white stripes and red spots on the head; some observed a straight tail or the feet.

I decided not to name the species for the children because our unexpected event presented a wonderful opportunity to do some research. As we entered the classroom, I quickly took out every field guide and bird book we owned. "Let's look through these books to find out about that bird," I suggested. Children worked alone or in pairs, and within minutes every group had found some type of woodpecker (hairy, downy, or the sapsucker).

After I read aloud a portion of an adult guide describing the peculiar pattern of holes drilled by a sapsucker (parallel, horizontal rows of holes), the children suggested that we go back to examine the holes. After looking at the holes, the children gleefully concluded that the unexpected visitor was indeed the sapsucker, a bird they had never heard of until that day. We also took a piece of the bark to study with a magnifying glass. Upon finding some tiny insects, one girl mused that perhaps the tree helps the bird by giving it food, and the bird helps the tree by taking the insects out of the tree—quite insightful for a kindergarten student!

As I listened to students' comments, I knew that the bird-watching study was not only spurring their interest in nature, but also helping them think in a scientific way.

Yearlong Benefits

Toward the end of the school year, one student's parent told me: "This past weekend, I looked out of the window and saw a bird. For fun, I asked my son what kind of bird it was. He studied the bird and told me it was a robin, commenting on the 'beautiful sound' of its chirp. I'm so pleased he is taking an interest in nature." This student's growing interest in birds had reached his family—the mother reported that they added bird feeders to their yard, selected a bird documentary to watch on television, and even visited the zoo to see exotic birds.

The yearlong bird study allowed time for planned lessons, such as our nature walk, and spontaneous events, such as the sapsucker investigation. Extended projects such as this one give children opportunities to develop proficiency with resources, create a wealth of written records, interpret a variety of maps and charts, and share knowledge gained with others. In these ways even young children can do the important work of science in a collaborative community.

Phyllis Whitin is an associate professor in the department of elementary and early childhood education at Queens College, CUNY, in Flushing, New York.

Resources

Doris, E. 1991. *Doing what scientists do.* Portsmouth, NH: Heinemann.

Gallas, K. 1995. *Talking their way into science.* New York: Teachers College.

National Research Council (NRC). 1996. *National Science Education Standards.* Washington, DC: National Academy Press.

Redding, J., P. Jacobs, C. McCrohon, and L. Herrenkohl. 1998. *Creating scientific communities in the elementary classroom.* Portsmouth, NH: Heinemann.

Ross, M. 1997. *Bird watching with Margaret Morse Nice.* Minneapolis, MN: Carolrhoda.

Stokes, D., and L. Stokes. 1996. *Stokes beginner's guide to birds.* Boston: Little, Brown.

Whitin, P., and D. Whitin. 1997. *Inquiry at the window: Pursuing the wonders of learners.* Portsmouth, NH: Heinemann.

Other Recommended Resources

Bash, B. 1992. *Urban roosts: Where birds nest in the city.* Boston: Little, Brown.

Ehlert, L. 1990. *Feathers for lunch.* New York: Scholastic.

Fichter, G. 1993. *Cardinals, robins, and other birds.* Racine, WI: Western.

Mazzola, F., Jr. 1997. *Counting is for the birds.* Watertown, MA: Charlesbridge.

Peterson, R.T. 1980. *Eastern birds.* Boston: Houghton Mifflin.

Silverstein, A., V. Silverstein, and R. Silverstein. 1994. *Eagles, hawks, and owls.* Boston: Little, Brown.

Tyrell, E. 1992. *Hummingbirds: Jewels of the sky.* New York: Crown.

Wood, A. 1997. *Birdsong.* New York: Harcourt, Brace.

Internet Resource

Cornell Lab of Ornithology. *birds.cornell.edu*

Tracking Through the Tulips

Both teachers and students had a wonderful time learning to do science as inquiry. The more we did, the easier it became.

Dorothy Davis

SAFETY NOTE

Make sure all students wash their hands after digging and handling tulip bulbs or any other plant.

Do you remember the song "Tiptoe Through the Tulips?" Kindergarten through second-grade students at Ashland City Primary in Ashland City, Tennessee, now do. It was their theme song as they participated in Journey North, a free, online educational program that enables students to track the blooming of tulips across the country as spring comes to North America (see "Internet Resources").

Not only did this unique program provide an exciting opportunity for online learning, it was also a perfect springboard for age-appropriate plant inquiries for all the students at the school. We thought tulips all year from fall through spring, and teachers were thrilled that the inquiries sparked students' enthusiasm for science and developed their knowledge of numerous science-process skills.

Aha! Tulips!

In fall 2002, teachers at our school were expressing interest in finding new ways to teach science as inquiry—and I was looking for an interesting plant inquiry for my second-grade students. That November, I attended a Journey North workshop at the Tennessee Science Teachers Association convention and had an aha moment: Journey North was the perfect vehicle to study plants, and not only for my students—it could involve the whole school in science inquiry.

I was quite excited at the prospect, talking up the Journey North idea to colleagues and eventually channeling my enthusiasm into a proposal for a Toyota Tapestry Grant that would provide the funds necessary for a schoolwide tulip investigation that I called Tracking Through the Tulips.

The idea was to create two tulip gardens on school grounds: a Journey North garden in which students would monitor tulips' growth and report data to the Journey North website and an "experimental" garden in which students could explore their own "what if...?" questions related to tulips. In addition, during the winter, students at each grade level would conduct age-appropriate investigations on potted tulips they forced indoors using grow lights. Through these experiences, all of the students would practice science inquiry, develop understandings of what is necessary for plants to grow, and begin to make connections about temperature, light, and plant growth.

Luckily, our proposal was reviewed favorably, and, in March 2003, we were awarded a $10,000 Tapestry Grant. The grant enabled the school to purchase computers and printers, tulips and other plant supplies, safety student thermometers, a grow light, Ohaus Triple Beam Balance, latitude maps of North America and compasses, and more—basically, everything we needed to get our tulip project off—or rather, *in*—the ground. Plus, we could keep the project going each year by just buying new tulip bulbs.

Laying the Groundwork

With the grant in hand, the next step was teacher training. In July 2003, I led a professional development workshop at the school explaining Tracking Through the Tulips, with the project implementation scheduled for fall 2003. At the training workshop, I showed a Journey North video that introduced the project. Teachers were given a Journey North tracking map, information on planting tulips, national and state standards the project would cover, soil investigation projects, history of tulips and art sheets depicting Holland, and information and activity sheets about animals and insects that consider tulips a food source. Teachers were excited to participate.

In September, when school began, the 15 teachers at my school were on board with the project and planning numerous tulip investigations they would conduct with their students. The state standards for each grade level guided the kind of inquiries each class would do. The inquiries with kindergarten students would involve learning about the care and growth of the tulip and learning how to read a thermometer. First-grade inquiries would develop those skills but add the skill of teaching children how to measure the growth of the tulip with a ruler. Second-grade students would conduct more in-depth inquiries—exploring the interrelationship of the tulips with the soil, animals, insects, temperature, and sunlight. They would also track "blooming dates" on a map as the tulips bloomed in North America and report their data online.

In all of the classes, students would examine a halved tulip bulb under a magnifying glass, keep a science journal, and draw pictures to help show what they had learned.

Planting Time

In the fall, the county agricultural extension agent introduced students to the project. Working with each grade level separately, he presented a play with the characters of tulip, water, different kinds of soil, and the Sun demonstrating how these elements work together to make the tulip grow. Then, he did a hands-on demonstration with different kinds of soil and answered questions about how to grow tulips.

Students learned that soil needs to be made of different-size particles so the water can flow through it slowly and the tulip bulb can get plenty of water but not stand in water. The agent sent our soil off to be tested, and we later found out that our soil needed compost to help the tulips grow well.

In November, the garden sites were plowed in preparation for planting. The gardens were near each other, but the experimental garden was shadier than the Journey North garden. Though teachers knew the amount of available light was a factor that would affect the blooming time of the tulips in this garden, we still believed it was important for students to have the opportunity to investigate their "what if" questions to further develop their inquiry skills.

Planting day—November 4—was completed in one day. Parent volunteers used bulb diggers to dig holes for the bulbs in the Journey North garden, which was about 7 m long and 3 m wide. The experimental garden was about half the size of the Journey North garden, and students dug their own holes at different depths according to their what-if questions. In both gardens, the students marked their tulips by inserting a tongue depressor with their names on it into the ground. In the experimental garden, students worked in groups of four, so they had to decide as a group how they would plant their tulips.

Each class had a designated area in the garden and was allotted 30 minutes to plant their bulbs. Before planting, students weighed their bulbs on a balance scale, measured the bulbs' circumference, and recorded the data in their science journals. This enabled us to compare bulbs before and after blooming, as students had such questions as, "Will the bulb weigh the same?" "Will it be the same shape?" and "Will it be the same color?"

Then, students planted the tulips. Make sure all students wash their hands after digging and handling tulip bulbs or any other plant. In the experimental garden, every tulip was planted with a different what-if question in mind:

- *What if* we planted it upside down? (kindergarten)
- *What if* we cut the tulip in half and planted it? (first grade)
- *What if* we placed wood on top of the bulb, would it still grow? (second grade)

Back in the classrooms, students reported data, such as the date and temperature, to the Journey North website and also recorded this data in their journals along with their questions and how they planted their bulbs.

All of the students also recorded their prediction of when they thought their tulip would bloom; these ranged from March through April. Overall, they thought the tulips in the experimental garden would bloom at the same time as those in the Journey North garden.

Bulb Dynamics

The day after we planted the tulips in the gardens outside, my second-grade students and I continued our investigations indoors by planting tulips in pots. My intention was to have students force them to bloom and through this process develop understandings that temperature and light affect blooming time.

Tulips require an approximately two-month cool period, so through November and December the potted bulbs were kept in a refrigerator at my home set at 5°C and kept moist. Then for about two weeks I kept them in my basement at home in front of a window so that they would gradually get used to light and increased temperature and begin to sprout before they were put under the grow light. The temperature was kept at 14°C and they were watered once a week.

By mid-January, the tulips had emerged, so on February 2 I brought the pots back to school and we continued investigating tulips, this time to explore the relationship that sunlight and temperature have on blooming time.

Tulips and Sunlight

"The Pattern of Sunlight on Our Tulips" centered on answering the question, "How can we get our potted tulips to bloom sooner?" —before March, the time we predicted our Journey North tulips would bloom.

Together, we determined our investigation question by first reviewing some of the temperature data we had collected so far in our tulip investigations. We looked at graphs of the temperatures at which we had kept our indoor potted tulips—Nov.–Dec. 5°C; Jan. 14°C; and Feb. 20°C—and graphs of the outside soil and air temperatures that we had recorded for the tulips in the Journey North garden.

Students observed that in the first part of February, it was cold and there were no sign of tulips emerging in the pots. Then, in the last half of February, it began to get warmer and the tulips began to emerge and grow.

Next, students looked at some things I had distributed to each of them before our discussion began: a potted tulip, a blank February calendar, and a March Farmer's Almanac calendar that predicted the month's weather and detailed each day's sunrise and sunset times.

I asked, "What is the Farmer's Almanac calendar telling us?" Students replied, "the weather—rainy, snowy, and cloudy." I said, "That is true, but what are those phrases really talking about?" I led students to the idea that those terms were referring to the presence of sunlight in addition to the temperature and precipitation. Then, I asked students, "Is there any way to tell how long the Sun is out each day?" and I pointed out that the March Almanac calendar tells the sunrise and sunset times each day. "Does anyone notice a pattern?" I asked.

One student said, "The times always change one number."

"Yes, the Sun rises one minute earlier and sets one minute later every day in March. There is more and more sunlight every day in spring."

One student wondered, "If you gave the tulip more light, would it grow faster?"

The question started the class thinking. I asked, "If tulips bloom in March when there is more light than in February, could we give our pots more light using our classroom's grow light and make them bloom faster?" Students were eager to try.

I told students we needed to figure out how much more light the tulips would be getting in March. They began to write the March sunrise and sunset times on their February calendar. They knew now that this was planning their experiment because they would be using these added daylight hours to set the timer on the grow light.

After the grow lights were set, students maintained the plants. Within two weeks, the first potted tulips bloomed—aptly it was February 13, the day of our Valentine party.

Several weeks after the tulips bloomed, we pulled the bulbs up and found "baby" tulips growing from the original bulbs. I explained these are called *bulblets* and that in a few years they might produce their own blooms. Students were excited to see that even though the tulip blooms had withered, there was new life growing under the soil.

Back to the Gardens

Students were thrilled to see the first tulip bloom in our Journey North garden on March 17. We reported this important event to the Journey North website. We used latitude maps of North America to help locate the different cities where the tulips were blooming. Then the students put a different color marker each week to track the blooming of the tulips. Weekly reports from the website helped the students track tulip blooms across the country and look for a pattern to how spring came to the United States.

For example, the tulips bloomed first around the southern coastlines of California, Texas, and South Carolina. Students remembered they had watched a Journey North video and learned the water along the coastline keeps the land warmer and that is why the tulips bloomed first along the coastlines.

Several weeks after our Journey North tulips began blooming, things started happening in the experimental garden, too. Students were walking around their tulips to see if they had emerged. Those who had planted their bulbs under pieces of wood were looking closely around the wood for signs of life.

Others saw the daffodils they had planted with their tulips come up around the tulips (when they bloomed, that was a pretty sight). Some were slower than others emerging and those students were getting worried. They were very concerned about their bulbs that were planted really deep or upside down because they had not emerged as quickly as some of the others, but when they finally emerged and bloomed, students were excited!

Tulips for Inquiry

We assessed student learning throughout the investigations. In students' science journals they wrote their questions, simple experiments, and results and compared and contrasted the indoor and outdoor plants and the Journey North and the experimental gardens. They wrote causes and effects of the different experiments. They drew, measured, weighed, graphed, and put into sequence the growth of the tulip.

In reflecting on our year of tulips, both teachers and students had a wonderful time learning to do science as inquiry. The more we did, the easier it became. The students' questions kept guiding the project and helped them get involved and have ownership of it. An unexpected outcome from Tracking Through the Tulips was that my wild second-grade class had become serious little scientists.

Dorothy Davis (Keri8davis@yahoo.com) *is a second-grade teacher at Ashland City Primary in Ashland City, Tennessee.*

Resources
Glattstein, J. and the National Gardening Association. 1998. *Flowering bulbs for dummies.* Chichester, UK: John Wiley and Sons.

National Research Council (NRC). 1996. *National Science Education Standards.* Washington, DC: National Academy Press.

Pranis, E., and J. Hale. 1988. *GrowLab: A complete guide to gardening in the classroom.* Burlington, VT: National Gardening Association.

Internet Resources

Forcing Tulip Bulbs
www.mrs.umn.edu/pyg/tips/perennials/tip_1502.shtml

Journey North
www.learner.org/jnorth

Toyota TAPESTY Grant Program
www.nsta.org/programs/tapestry

Connecting to the Standards

This article relates to the following National Science Education Standards (NRC 1996):

Content Standards
Grades K–4

Standard A: Science as Inquiry
- Abilities necessary to do scientific inquiry

Standard C: Life Science
- The characteristics of organisms
- Life cycles of organisms
- Organisms and environment

Standard D: Earth and Space Science
- Objects in the sky
- Changes in Earth and sky

The Science and Mathematics of Building Structures

Preschool students develop inquiry skills as they investigate how high they can build.

Ingrid Chalufour, Cindy Hoisington, Robin Moriarty, Jeff Winokur, and Karen Worth

Imagine preschool children playing with blocks—nothing unusual about that, right? Well, now imagine these children using blocks to conduct a rich science inquiry that integrates mathematics and science skills—from exploring shape, pattern, measurement, and spatial relationships to developing understandings of stability, balance, and properties of materials. Sound impossible? It's not.

Students in a Head Start program in Boston did just that, and the success of their learning experience was inspiring. Their teacher and a group of curriculum developers who worked with her as she conducted this integrated unit wrote this article to share their story and thoughts. Through this classroom's experience, you will see that you can use everyday activities—like building blocks—as a basis for meaningful learning that meets national educational standards in science and mathematics.

Identifying the Standards

The idea for the integrated unit came about as we reflected on the science that normally took place in the teacher's classroom and realized that neither the science table, with its collection of shells, bird nests, and magnets, nor the planned activities, such as mixing cornstarch and water, were engaging students in rich science inquiries—inquiries that would give students reasons to measure, count, or look for patterns. The children loved to build, and as we talked together, the potential for integrating science and mathematics in block play became clear. We started by identifying some developmentally appropriate concepts that could be the focus of the children's block play.

In science, we identified stability, balance, and properties of materials as concepts to explore. In mathematics, we identified numbers and operations as concepts students would use as they collected data about their structures.

In addition to these discipline-specific concepts, we identified several concepts and processes that were part of both the science and mathematics standards. For example, standards in both science and mathematics identify shape, pattern, measurement, and spatial relationships as important concepts for study. Similarly, both disciplines identify questioning, problem solving, analyzing, reasoning, communicating, connecting, investigating, and creating and using representations as processes central to engagement with each subject.

Together we created a Venn diagram (Figure 1) to clarify our thinking and to show the relationships between the content and processes presented in *National Science Education Standards* (NRC 1996) and

National Council of Teachers of Mathematics Principles and Standards for School Mathematics (NCTM 2000). The figure's center area points out the unit's areas of overlap, while the areas on the right- and left-hand sides point out the targeted concepts specific to each discipline.

Readying the Classroom

Having identified the standards that would guide the teaching and learning in the block unit over the next several months, the teacher set about transforming the classroom to best meet the unit's learning goals and the needs and interests of her students.

To begin, she created an environment for inquiry by enlarging the block area, creating additional building centers and add-

Figure 1. This Venn diagram highlights the unit's relationships between science and math content and processes.

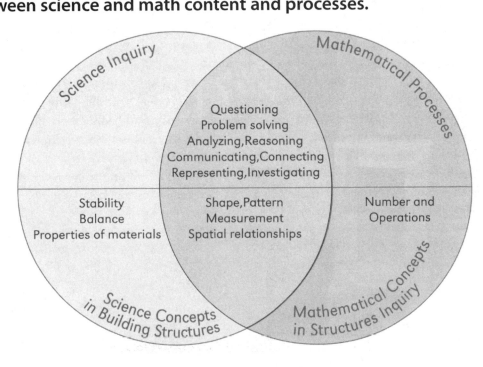

ing foam and cardboard blocks to the collection of unit, hollow, and tabletop blocks. She also temporarily removed Lego's from the block collection. Though the children loved Lego's, they tended to use them to build solid, squat structures, and she wanted them to experiment with materials that did not stick together. She hoped the other kinds of blocks would entice students to explore the relationship between the kind of materials they used for building and the balance and stability of their structures. The Lego's would be reintroduced later in the exploration so students could compare them to the other building materials.

In addition to changes in the block areas, the teacher displayed books and posters of structures around the classroom, such as the Eiffel Tower, the Empire State Building, and various other buildings and bridges. For easier access to the blocks and to facilitate cleanup, she labeled shelves with pictures of each kind of block, which provided students the added benefit of practicing their problem-solving skills as they compared shapes and their attributes.

Before the unit began, we all worked with the blocks to explore how they balanced and how different designs and kinds of materials affected structures' stability. This experimentation was a big help when the classroom teacher later observed students' block play to consider the mathematics and science concepts they were exploring.

Open Exploration

Twenty-four children, speaking eight different languages, arrived in the classroom in mid-September. For the first month of school, the teacher's goal was to engage students in building and provide opportunities for students to wonder, question, and develop initial understandings of properties of materials, stability, and balance.

Every day students explored, via trial and error, what the materials could and could not do. They discovered quite a bit about their triangle-shaped blocks. For example, they determined it's possible but not easy to balance a rectangular-shaped block on the point of a triangular one; they noticed that two triangular blocks together can be used instead of one square block, but only if the triangular blocks are laid on their flat sides. They agreed that triangular blocks are not strong when you try to stand them up as a square: the two triangles slip away from each other.

Every day at the class's morning meeting, the teacher got students excited about using the building materials. She talked about the children's buildings or drawings from the previous day's block play and then shared a picture of an interesting building (the Taj Mahal, for example) or introduced a new kind of building material.

During the daily choice time or activity time (about an hour each day), the children worked in three block centers. During this time, the teacher walked around the classroom, observing the different ways children built and expressing interest in students' block play. She asked children to tell her about their buildings, described interesting features of their structures aloud, and sketched and photographed children's buildings.

Toward the end of each week, she engaged children in talking about the patterns and designs they were using. These weekly science talks helped children articulate, examine, and defend their developing ideas about how to build strong buildings: what materials were best, and which blocks were good at the bottom.

To stimulate these conversations, the teacher referred to the drawings and photographs and to excerpts from conversations she'd had with children about their structures' stability—for example, "You need to use big blocks on the bottom and smaller ones on top if you want to have a strong building" or "If it starts to wiggle, you need to hold it with your hands."

As students became more comfortable with their building experiences, the teacher began to highlight the science and mathematics in her children's open exploration of building structures.

She used comments like "The block under your house makes for a strong foundation" and "The block between these walls is balancing on its end" to focus attention on the structures' designs and stability and relative position in space. In so doing, she addressed a section of the NCTM geometry standard as she modeled vocabulary—such as *under* and *between*—that children need to learn as they talk about location and space.

As she communicated her interest in the ways children had designed and balanced their structures, the teacher supported each child's development of new science and mathematics language and modeled its use. This enabled the children to communicate better with one another, an element of both the NSES and the NCTM's communication standards.

Questioning and Investigating

A few weeks into the open exploration of building structures, the teacher noticed students' preoccupation with building straight up. She decided to help students focus their inquiry on the question they all seemed to be asking through their building behavior: How tall can we build?

She brought the children together and showed them photographs of the towers they'd been building out of different kinds of blocks. She articulated their question, "How tall can we build?," and asked for predictions.

Some children used movement, some used numbers, and others described height in terms of other objects ("as tall as the door," for example) to answer how tall they could build. The teacher recorded students' ideas in words, numerals, and sketches, and she helped interested groups and individuals plan their investigation by working with them to figure out who was going to build where during the upcoming choice time. Children could select in which of the three different building centers they were going to work. Some children partnered up; others worked solo.

Now that the children's science investigation focused on a single question, the teacher facilitated this part of the inquiry differently. She used morning meetings for the next few weeks to refer children to the previous day's data, plan their day's work, or make predictions about what they might discover.

During choice times, she encouraged children to represent their towers' heights in two dimensions and three dimensions, and she helped them measure their towers, count the blocks, and compare heights. She used the weekly science talks to help students analyze their data and support their developing theories about building tall towers with evidence from their own experiences.

In one science talk, for example, the teacher shared photos and representations of the children's towers and, together, they compared the numbers of blocks on towers of different sizes. Students were able to easily observe that the taller towers had more blocks.

In another talk, students discussed which kinds of blocks—unit blocks or cardboard blocks—made the tallest towers. The teacher asked students probing questions, such as "Why do you think the cardboard blocks fell down more than these cylinders?," to encourage students to elaborate on their ideas. In this way, the teacher was able to shift the children's focus from the effects of design on their towers' height and stability to the effects of the properties of the building materials themselves on the stability of a tall structure.

As she worked with her class, the teacher deepened students' science and mathematics learning in several ways. For example, she
- identified questions to focus the inquiry;
- helped children collect data using photographs, drawings, models, counting, and measuring;
- used informal conversations and whole-group science talks to help children communicate and analyze their data; and
- encouraged students to use representations and other data to articulate theories they developed about how design and properties of materials affect a tower's stability.

By encouraging students to articulate theories and use evidence from their work to support their ideas she also addressed NCTM's process standards: reasoning and proof; data analysis and probability; and communication. Children also measured and counted with a purpose: to collect data that would help them answer their questions, "How tall can we build?" and "Which blocks make the tallest towers?"

Tying It Together

As the children's interest in building tall towers began to wane, the teacher suggested they hold an open house so they could share their investigation of the ways materials and designs affect tall structures' stability.

When the visitors came, students challenged their guests to build tall, stable structures. They passed out clipboards and markers and invited the guests to draw their structures and write about the strategies they'd used to make their structures stable. Photographs, charts, and documentation panels were hung around the classroom, and the teacher encouraged the visitors to ask the children about them.

The teacher also referred to the experience and shared examples of students' work in parent-teacher conferences to discuss how their children's social and emotional, language, and mathematical skills and understandings had developed in concert with their developing understanding of inquiry, stability, balance, and properties of materials.

Beyond Blocks

Building with blocks clearly offered this teacher and her students rich opportunities to integrate mathematics and science. Other science topics can also offer similar opportunities.

For example, try adapting the Venn diagram to facilitate a life science inquiry, such as a study of organisms in the environment (see Figure 1). Replace the physical science concepts related to building structures, currently listed in the bottom left-hand section of the diagram, with age-appropriate concepts related to life science, such as life cycle, characteristics of living things, and habitat.

Think about a rich classroom environment including many plants representing a good variety and several terrariums representing different local habitats. Think about taking children outdoors each day to observe their natural surroundings. Try to fill out the rest of the Venn diagram.

You might include opportunities for three-, four-, and five-year olds to use patterning, counting, measuring, and spatial relationships to describe what children notice and think about the growth and development of living things. With a little consideration, it is possible to create integrated science and mathematics units that keep the integrity of each subject and also highlight the overlapping processes and concepts central to both subjects.

Ingrid Chalufour is a project director with the Center for Children and Families at Education Development Center (EDC) in Newton, Massachusetts; Cindy Hoisington was a classroom teacher at Action Boston Community Development South Side Head Start in Roslindale, Massachusetts, when she helped develop the activities discussed in this article; Robin Moriarty (rmoriarty@edc.org) is a curriculum developer in the Center for Science Education (CSE) at EDC; Jeff Winokur is a senior research associate at CSE and an instructor at Wheelock College in Boston, Massachusetts; and Karen Worth is a senior scientist in CSE and a graduate level instructor, also at Wheelock College.

Resources

National Council of Teachers of Mathematics (NCTM). 2000. *Principles and standards for school mathematics.* Reston, VA: Author.

National Research Council (NRC). 1996. *National Science Education Standards.* Washington, DC: National Academy Press.

Connecting to the Standards

This article relates to the following National Science Education Standards (NRC 1996):

Content Standards
Grades K–4

Standard A: Science as Inquiry

- Abilities necessary to do scientific inquiry

Standard B: Physical Science

- Properties of objects and materials
- Position and motion of objects

This article relates to the following Principles and Standards for School Mathematics (NCTM 2000):

Grades PreK–12

Algebra

- Understand patterns, relations, and functions

Geometry

- Analyze characteristics and properties of two- and three-dimensional geometric shapes and develop mathematical arguments about geometric relationships
- Use visualization, spatial reasoning, and geometric modeling to solve problems

Data Analysis and Probability

- Formulate questions that can be addressed with data and collect, organize, and display relevant data to answer them

Communication

- Organize and consolidate their mathematical thinking through communication

Connections

- Recognize and apply mathematics in contexts outside of mathematics

Representation

- Create and use representations to organize, record, and communicate mathematical ideas

Discovery Central

Through the learning centers, my students had experienced science in a personal way that provided a sense of accomplishment.

Jaimee Wood

Spring is an exciting time in my—or any—kindergarten classroom. The children are communicating better, and they have begun working more independently. Their critical-thinking skills are growing each day.

Last year, as the warm days of spring teased our senses, a plant unit seemed especially enticing, so I created four interactive, plant-themed learning centers that developed science-process skills, including observing, comparing, recording data, collecting data, sorting, and classifying.

The centers addressed four curriculum areas—mathematics, fine arts, communication arts, and science, and they incorporated the use of a journal in which students wrote or drew every day, further developing students' improving communication skills. Though the tasks at each center embraced different parts of the curriculum, they all related to plants and gave children a chance to get their hands dirty and experience the joy of discovery and exploration—an important goal of our kindergarten science curriculum.

Although I developed plant-themed learning centers, the approach can be used effectively with nearly any topic, and I encourage you to try learning centers with your students. The lessons at our centers came from my local curriculum, the AIMS book *Primarily Plants* (Hoover and Mercier 1990), and Successlink—a Missouri Department of Education website where educators share teaching ideas (see "Internet Resources").

Where Do We Start?

Before preparing the centers, I did a preassessment to find out what students knew about plants. I asked students to write down the four most important things that plants need. Some ideas students listed were *family, homes, dirt, water, bugs,* and *food.* Their answers told me I had a lot of work to accomplish in this unit.

My objective with the learning centers was to help students build background knowledge about plants and practice their science-process skills. First, I wanted to find out what my students knew about plants and what they wanted to learn about plants.

Together the class created a KWL chart ("What I Know," "What I Want to Know," and "What I Learned"). Students **K**new "plants grow everywhere," "plants are green," "plants don't eat food," and "plants are in dirt." They **W**anted to know the following:

- Why are plants green?
- How do plants grow?
- Do plants need water?
- Are flowers plants? and
- Do all plants have leaves?

This chart became a great learning tool throughout the unit: As students discovered new information about plants, we referred back to our KWL chart and recorded their findings on the "What I **L**earned" part of the chart.

Sorting Seeds

At the first center, I provided chart paper, small paper cups, a hand lens, and assorted seeds: lima beans, kidney beans, popcorn, sunflower seeds, garbanzo beans, and black-eyed peas. Students counted the seeds and then grouped the seeds by recognizable traits, such as color, size, shape, and texture.

The students estimated how many seeds it would take to balance one teddy bear. They then weighed the seeds and recorded their results.

Finally, students made drawings of the seeds in their journals and recorded their observations and questions, such as "Will all of these seeds grow?" and "Why are the seeds different colors?"

An extension of this activity is to plant the seeds so students can answer such questions as "Which seed will sprout first?"

Painting With Nature

The art center followed a brief lesson on the plant parts in which students learned that the stem supports the upper parts of the plant; the roots anchor the plants in the soil; the flowers are the reproductive parts of the plants; and the leaves are the part of the plant where food is made.

At this center, the objective was to reinforce students' knowledge of plant parts by painting a plant using items from nature. I provided various items from nature—flowers with stems, pinecones, leaves, corncobs, and celery stalks along with paint, paper, and easels.

"How do we paint without paintbrushes?" was the response I heard from my kindergartners at the art center. I encouraged the students to use their imagination and be creative and showed them one example using a celery stalk.

The children were asked to include the correct plant parts in their plant painting and to identify the parts of the plants with which they painted—such as the leaf. Afterward, we displayed plant posters around the room and at the center to help students remember the new names they had learned.

Listening and Writing

At this center, students started out by listening to stories about plants (see "Resources"). Next, they illustrated their favorite parts of the books and explained their illustrations on paper and orally.

Students also completed a booklet from AIMS called "What Do Plants Need to Grow?" (see "Internet Resources"). Students colored and decorated the booklet as they wished. The book started with "plants need soil," and then continued to add a plant need on each page.

Planting Seeds

Now it was time for the students to predict and experiment with their own plant. The objective of the final center was for students to watch a bean seed grow. I gave each student a small clay pot or Styrofoam cup, potting soil, and a bean seed.

Students planted their seeds and chose a spot in the room to place their plants. They were instructed not to move their pots during the growth period. I wanted them to see that seeds grow when the conditions are right.

Students also wrote in their science journals many times during this process. The students illustrated the growth process of their plants every day in their journals. I asked them to include anything they did to their plant, such as watering and measuring.

Sprouting Knowledge

After completing all of the learning centers, we talked about all we had learned about what plants need to grow. Students had observed that plants need sunlight and water through their growing experiment.

The kindergarten classroom is a safe and familiar environment in which students can develop the scientific skills of observing, sorting and organizing, comparing, predicting, experimenting, evaluating, and applying. Science centers help build students' self-esteem by giving them hands-on experiences. Students were given time to familiarize themselves with the materials at each center, encouraged to make their own observations, and allowed to proceed at their own learn-

ing pace, giving them a sense of control and ownership while exploring science.

Through the learning centers, my students had experienced science in a personal way that provided a sense of accomplishment and gave them wonderful memories of their kindergarten class, too.

Jaimee Wood (jwood@laplata.k12.mo.us) *is a kindergarten teacher at La Plata R-II School District in La Plata, Missouri.*

Resources

Carle, E. 1991. *The tiny seed.* New York: Simon and Schuster.

Ehlert, L. 1987. *Growing vegetable soup.* New York: Harcourt.

Hoover, E., and S. Mercier. 1990. *Primarily plants.* Fresno, CA: AIMS Education Foundation.

National Research Council (NRC). 1996. *National Science Education Standards.* Washington, DC: National Academy Press.

Internet Resources
AIMS
www.aimsedu.org

Successlink
www.successlink.org

Connecting to the Standards
This article relates to the following National Science Education Standards (NRC 1996):

Content Standards
Grades K–4

Standard C: Life Science
- The characteristics of organisms
- Life cycles of organisms
- Organisms and environments

Ladybugs Across the Curriculum

Scientific inquiry and Howard Gardner's theory of multiple intelligences converge as a kindergarten class explores the world of ladybugs.

Christina Dias Ward and Michael J. Dias

When Azrin, a student in my kindergarten class, brought a ladybug to school for show and tell, it was the center of attention all day long. The children posed many questions: "What do ladybugs eat?" "When do they fly?" "How long does a ladybug live?"

My brother, a science education professor, and I often talk to each other about what's happening in our classrooms. We realized we had an opportunity on our hands, and our ladybug project—a thematic unit centered on the study of that beloved beetle—was born. We planned these experiences together, and I implemented them in my kindergarten classroom.

The day after show and tell, I ordered live specimens for the class (see box on p. 99). A few weeks later, 100 ladybugs arrived. We placed them in their lodge, a cardboard house with viewing windows on all sides, and the children took on the role of entomologists, studying live specimens as active investigators. For the next two weeks, the children used magnifying glasses, observation tubes, and mirrors to predict, hypothesize, classify, measure, and observe the ladybugs in action.

This cross-curricular experience also offered the children the opportunity to have their unique learning preferences addressed. Students chose their favorite learning centers and expressed their knowledge of ladybugs using the multiple intelligences: verbal-linguistic, logical-mathematical, visual-spatial, bodily kinesthetic, musical, interpersonal, intrapersonal, and naturalist (Gardner 1983).

A Range of Talents

Believing that all children should have their multiple intelligences nurtured, we planned and implemented a set of learning experiences that would engage each of these capacities for the children in this kindergarten classroom (see Figure 1). Our study of ladybugs gave children the opportunity to learn in at least eight different ways—all students had their strongest intelligences addressed at least some of the time.

Figure 1. The various ways multiple intelligences were addressed through the ladybug project.

Verbal-Linguistic	Daily observation and discovery journal; ladybug books; listening centers; class discussion; labeling chart; publication of class book, *What We Know About Ladybugs*.
Logical-Mathematical	Counting and estimating number of ladybugs in the lodge; sharing counting strategies; comparison and measurement.
Visual-Spatial	Drawing, visualizing, designing color illustrations; reading life cycle diagrams; using flow charts and flip charts to present learning.
Bodily Kinesthetic	Hands-on investigation; role-playing; ladybug construction; puzzles and manipulatives; dance.
Musical	Recognizing and reproducing rhythmic patterns; creating short chants, songs, and raps.
Interpersonal	Peer sharing at the lodge; using think-pair-share strategies; generating testable questions.
Intrapersonal	Quiet reflection in the reading house; writing in journal; providing many choices and interest centers.
Naturalist	Exploring, seeking, and identifying patterns; classifying varieties and life cycle phases; observing organisms in classroom and nature.

Most educators are familiar with Howard Gardner's theory of multiple intelligences (1983, 1991). Gardner's view of intelligence recognizes the merit of the traditional emphasis on verbal and mathematical prowess but embraces a much broader array of intellectual capacities. For example, educators in agreement with the notion of multiple intelligences build upon learner aptitudes in the musical, bodily kinesthetic, visual-spatial, personal, and other areas and appreciate the way Gardner's theory affirms a wider range of student talents and abilities.

Ladybug Literacy

Linguistic intelligence involves the use of words, both written and spoken. The ladybugs provided many opportunities for communication and research. Each child kept a journal that included daily observations and discoveries. Our book center was full of books about ladybugs (see "Ladybug Bibliography," p. 100) that we read together each day and that children read independently. Children could choose ladybug stories, such as *The Grouchy Ladybug* by Eric Carle (1986), to hear at the listening center.

Class discussions were sparked by our new findings—for example, one student noted one morning the ladybugs were asleep in a clump in a corner of their lodge. Another student recalled a book that said ladybugs were sociable and even hibernated in groups. A class favorite was the big chart on which children could label the parts of a ladybug, from antennae to wing case. After the release of the ladybugs, the class published a book called *What We Know About Ladybugs*—still a daily choice for independent reading months later.

Ladybug Mathematics

Logical-mathematical intelligence focuses on numbers, calculations, logic, classifications, and critical-thinking skills. When the ladybugs arrived, the children were not told how many were in the lodge. Over the two-week period, children counted, estimated, and wrote their guesses on a piece of paper. A few ladybugs died, and others escaped into our room, which complicated the calculations. Students shared their ways of solving the problem and strategies for counting efficiently, such as chunking the ladybug lodge into areas and making the problem smaller; working with a partner who counted out loud while the other tallied on paper; and counting when the ladybugs were asleep.

Because each of our ladybugs was about the size of a split pea, we used peas in our math center to represent the ladybugs. Questions were posed to the children, such as, "How many ladybugs could fit on a spoon? In a jar lid? In a cup?" Using split peas, the students made predictions, tested their guesses, and recorded their results. Even now, months after the ladybug release,

---

Ladybug Learning Center— Here's how to do it!

Order ladybugs and lodge from Insect Lore (1-800-LIVE-BUG; *www.insectlore.com*).

Ladybugs can also be purchased from local garden stores. Another option for a ladybug lodge is a clear container with mesh screening that securely covers the opening. Caution: Ladybugs can squeeze through tiny slits or openings—we found ladybugs all over our classroom! A small stick or twig placed at an angle allows ladybugs to climb and explore inside the lodge. Feed ladybugs two to three raisins soaked in water daily. Fold a paper napkin or paper towel and place it on the floor of your ladybug lodge. Squeeze a small eyedropper full of water on it each day. If you have access to aphid-infested leaves, the ladybugs would love them.

---

children use split peas to measure in "ladybugs"—"Our table is 162 ladybugs across!"

No Two Ladybugs Are Alike

Visual-spatial intelligence invites children to draw, visualize, imagine, and use color. Visual art served as a primary vehicle for the children to express what they learned about ladybugs. Colorful illustrations and drawings in their published book were powerful expressions of learning and scientific thinking. The ladybug parts students had been so busy labeling and observing appeared in their drawings: six legs, wing cases, wings, thorax, abdomen, and antennae.

Picture literacy experiences involve spatial intelligence. While the students learned about the life cycle of ladybugs, pictures clearly told the story. Relying on our large life-cycle poster in the front of the room, we drew pictures on the board depicting a ladybug at various stages to generate questions and lead to discussion. As the days of our study progressed, children demonstrated their knowledge through pictures; their own sequential renderings of a ladybug's life included flow charts, circular patterns, arrows and boxes, and miniflip charts—all chock-full of their sketches and personal graphic symbols.

Most kindergarten students cannot write papers about their learning: They use art as one of their prime languages. The children researched ladybugs by listening to me read many nonfiction books about ladybugs and by examining ladybug books during independent reading times. Using brown lunch bags, pipe cleaners, paper scraps, and paint, each child created a ladybug and conveyed what he or she had learned. For example, the children were intrigued with the knowledge that not all ladybugs were red with spots. They learned some ladybugs are orange, some are yellow, some are combinations of these colors, some have many spots, and some have no spots at all. This information was reflected in their art. No two ladybugs were alike, yet each reflected a specific species or variety of ladybug.

Dance of the Ladybugs

Bodily kinesthetic intelligence is the ability to involve the whole body or use hands-on experiences to solve a problem, create something, or put on some kind of production. All young children need to move to learn, but for those who are exceptionally strong in bodily kinesthetic intelligence, movement

Ladybug Bibliography

Nonfiction Titles

Allen, J., and T. Humphries. 2000. *Are You a ladybug?* New York: Kingfisher.

Bailey, J. 1989. *The life cycle of a ladybug.* New York: Bookwright.

Braithwaite, A. 1989. *Ladybugs.* Life Cycle Books. Chicago: Dearborn.

Fischer-Nagel, H. 1986. *Life of the ladybug.* Minneapolis, MN: Carolrhoda.

Jeuness, G., and P. Bourgoiing. 1989. *The Ladybug and other insects: A first discovery book.* New York: Scholastic.

Watts, B. 1987. *Ladybug.* Morristown, NJ: Silver Burdett.

Fiction Titles

Brown, R. 1988. *Ladybug, ladybug.* New York: Dutton.

Carle, E. 1986. *The grouchy ladybug.* New York: Thomas Crowell.

Cutting, B., and J. Cutting. 1988. *Are you a ladybug?* Bothell, WA: Wright Group.

Schlein, M. 1953. *Fast is not a ladybug.* Reading, MA: Addison-Wesley.

is imperative. During our ladybug experience, the students had many opportunities to move, work with their hands, and role-play.

In addition to the art they had already created, many children chose to construct ladybugs at our Creation Station. This center contained construction paper, clay, boxes, cardboard, Styrofoam, pipe cleaners, and other materials discarded from other projects. By building with different materials, children could move around and use their hands to internalize how the parts relate to the whole ladybug. Similar thinking occurred as children put together ladybug puzzles or used manipulatives like Lego's to build ladybugs.

The class was fascinated with the way the ladybugs moved around during the day and bunched up at night to sleep. Students were also curious about the process of *molting*, in which the exoskeleton is shed to allow the insect to grow. It seemed a logical next step to stand up and act out what we had researched and observed. Children exuberantly wiggled and molted and shed and grew. They asked for music "to fly to" and called it the "Dance of the Ladybugs" as they fluttered around the room. They curled their bodies in little balls close to their friends to simulate how ladybugs hibernate during the winter.

Finally, good literature provided a springboard for role-play experiences. This group never tired of taking on the roles in Eric Carle's *The Grouchy Ladybug*. Ladybug hand and finger puppets were available for students to use as props in their dramatic play or storytelling.

Ladybug Rap

Musical intelligence is the capacity to hear patterns in music and rhythms, recognize them, reproduce them, and even manipulate them. Most young children respond positively to music, silly songs, and rhythms; many times, the best way to teach a concept, skill, or habit is to make up a song about it.

Every morning in our classroom, we sing a good morning song that incorporates each child's happy news. During our study of ladybugs, children would share observations and we would sing about these ("Our ladybugs drank up their water, What a happy day ....").

Most fun of all was listening to these rhythmically charged kindergarteners create miniraps about ladybugs, such as this:
I am a ladybug and I'm here to say
I eat aphids every day!

Learning Is Social

Interpersonal intelligence involves understanding other people and possessing the ability to relate to them. Learning is a social process, and most young children enjoy interacting with others. The Ladybug Lodge Center was a social event each day, as children observed with magnifiers and talked to each other about what they saw. This peer sharing was a rich source of knowledge that was discussed and recorded as a whole group.

Think-pair-share strategies provided time for pairs of children to think about a question first, talk about their ideas with their partner, and then share them with the class. Questions children posed included: "How big is a ladybug's stomach?" "Can a ladybug see in color?" and "How far can a ladybug fly before landing?" Entomologists from local agencies or universities can provide answers to difficult questions and reinforce the notion that learning is a social process—we are all teachers and learners.

Reflection Time

Intrapersonal intelligence refers to having a good understanding of self. In our fast-paced world, children need time to reflect and think about what they have heard and observed. Every classroom needs a quiet place to go to get away from everyone—in our room it is the reading house. Children choose this spot to listen to recordings of their favorite stories, curl up on the rug with a favorite book, or just be alone. This spot was used many times by individual students during the ladybug study to construct ladybug puzzles, write in their journals, or read one of the many ladybug books. Keeping a journal about the ladybug process provided an outlet for personal expression, feelings, and insights for each child.

Intrapersonal intelligence is nurtured in a classroom that provides many choices and interest centers for children. Observing a child make choices, pursue a task, make decisions, and solve problems yields a wealth of information for teachers. More important, it provides self-knowledge for the child—autonomy, confidence, independence, and an "I can do it" attitude.

Knowing Nature

Naturalist intelligence is a person's ability to identify and classify patterns in nature and their sensitivity to features in the natural world. The outdoors becomes the classroom, as young children are encouraged to explore, classify, look for patterns, and discover.

The ladybug study provided ample outdoor exploration. Before our ladybugs arrived, we looked on our school grounds for ladybugs and found a few under leaves and on trees. We compared these to our shipment, and found they were a different species.

Additional nature walks yielded better predictions of where to find ladybugs. A week after all ladybugs were released, we went on a ladybug hunt outdoors to see if we could find any of ours. The children were thrilled to see so many ladybugs still hanging around our school.

Nurturing Intelligences

Designing experiences in which children explore, gather evidence, and formulate explanations is teaching science as inquiry. Such learning experiences seem quite amenable to the integration of each of Gardner's multiple intelligences. We look forward to hearing about your creative science inquiry lessons and how they nurture the many forms of intelligences your students bring to the classroom.

Christina Dias Ward (cward5448@comcast.net) *is a kindergarten teacher at Granbery Elementary School in Nashville, Tennessee. Michael J. Dias is an assistant professor of science education at Kennesaw State University in Kennesaw, Georgia.*

Resources

Armstrong, T. 1994. *Multiple intelligences in the classroom.* Alexandria, VA: Association for Supervision and Curriculum Development.

Gardner, H. 1983. *Frames of mind.* New York: Basic.

Gardner, H. 1991. *The unschooled mind: How children think and how schools should teach.* New York: Bantam.

National Research Council (NRC). 1996. *National Science Education Standards.* Washington, DC: National Academy Press.

Connecting to the Standards

This article relates to the following National Science Education Standards (NRC 1996):

Content Standards

Grades K–4

Standard A: Science as Inquiry

- Abilities necessary to do scientific inquiry

Standard C: Life Science

- The characteristics of organisms
- Life cycles of organisms
- Organisms and their environment

Miniature Sleds, Go, Go, Go!

These hands-on, action-oriented problem solvers are walking, talking engineers just ready to explore, build, and discover.

Gina A. Sarow

Imagine kindergartners eagerly creating blueprints for their own inventions. Imagine them actually building them with tools. Now imagine them testing out their design and explaining the science behind it to their peers. Not possible, you say? It is with *Design Technology: Children's Engineering* (Dunn and Larson 1990), a learning model I implemented in my classroom two years ago. This model allows children to experience developmentally appropriate, hands-on instructional methods that enable them to draw, plan, design, build, test, and improve their solutions by applying their knowledge to new and different situations.

Engineering and design technology is not a separate subject but rather a supplement to classroom lessons. In my classroom, I began incorporating one design technology lesson each month to coincide with such themes as plants, bugs, and the weather, and it worked beautifully. We always began with a related children's literature story—thanks to our wonderful librarians—and branched out to other areas of curriculum, such as science, mathematics, writing, and art.

Examples of engineering projects I've done with students include building a sailboat that sails in a wind channel, building a bug catcher to take home and catch live bugs, and designing a snake whose both ends move. One of the most successful engineering and design activities I've conducted with students was a miniature sled-building activity that resulted from a brainstorming session among two teachers and myself.

A Sledding Party

The sledding project began after a huge snowfall (20–25 cm) one November. I took the children to the library and read aloud *The 14 Forest Mice and the Winter Sledding Day* by Kazuo Iwamura (1991), which relates how a father mouse kept his little mice busy during the long snow season by planning, drawing, and building sleds. In our Wisconsin community, the wind chill often makes it feel as though the temperature is below freezing, so children usually have to stay indoors. I challenged the children to build a miniature sled that would go down a hill carrying weight—this was our way of keeping busy like the mice.

Soon after reading the story, I sent home a newsletter about the sled activity and asked parents to help their children bring their sleds to school for a sledding party the next day. (Sleds are not allowed on school buses for safety reasons.) Parents brought in an assortment of sleds, including cardboard sleds, wooden toboggans, and plastic sleds and saucers. One child's mother brought in a catalog flier showing different types of sleds on sale at a local store, and another parent contributed an article from the newspaper about what makes a good sled.

It was a beautiful day for sledding: The sun was out, the air was warm, and the snow was tightly packed from snowmobiles traveling to school. After an afternoon of sledding, the children and I sipped hot chocolate with marshmallows, which provided a great opportunity for the children to talk about what materials worked best for sledding and why. They discussed their sleds in groups of two so that they could bounce ideas off each other, an important concept when beginning open-ended lessons for kindergarten children.

The children reached a consensus that a good sled was one that moves fast. Some children thought metal would make the sleds go the fastest because snowmobiles have metal skis—many students have older siblings who drive snowmobiles to school. One child said the speed could come from the same power—weight and gravity—we used in building fire trucks—a previous engineering project. Others discussed using plastic for their sleds because many of them used plastic sleds and saucers at home.

In the winter When there's snow We get our sleds And away we go!

Classroom Construction Site

Materials for the sleds and the space to build them came from our classroom construction site, where students regularly practiced with tools and made their own designs. At the beginning of the year, I sought help from parents and other volunteers to build a construction center in our classroom, supplied with recycled materials of every shape and kind for projects. I sent home an initial newsletter asking parents and relatives to save various boxes, paper-towel tubes, plastic foam, thread spools, milk cartons, egg cartons, fabric, milk caps, plastic caps from peanut butter jars, buttons, wood scraps, duct tape, and aluminum pie tins. Parents were enthusiastic about the construction center and contributed a wide range of materials, including oatmeal boxes, wheels and gears from nearby factories, and colored wire from the local phone company. Parent volunteers organized these materials in plastic stocking shelves in the classroom.

Students used this construction center throughout the year for all of their engineering and design projects. I purchased tools that were just the right size for very

Figure 1. Student Blueprint Examples.

Our Sled Blueprint

Partners: CLTON SHSE MLY

Challenge: To build a sled that will slide down a hill of snow while carrying weight.

Our Sled Blueprint

Partners: mhe and JlP

Challenge: To build a sled that will slide down a hill of snow while carrying weight.

young children using funds from the Herb Kohl Educational Foundation. (I was a Kohl Teacher Fellowship recipient.) Criteria for tool size were based on the children's sizes and their experience using such tools.

Tool Safety

Parents also volunteered to teach tool safety. During class visits, they showed the children various tools, taught the correct name for each tool, and demonstrated how each tool was used in an appropriate manner. During these sessions the parents practiced building with the children. While making a simple hat hanger, for example, parents showed the class how high to swing a hammer—never higher than your shoulder, for control—and how to use the reamer—hand tool for enlarging 3/16″ holes.

The construction center enabled students to develop and practice the skills required for construction. Many teachers, administrators, and parents may feel apprehensive at the thought of young children using such tools as small hammers, hole punchers, and vises. I feel, however, that if children are given the appropriate-size tools for their small hands and shown how to use them correctly, they quickly develop the fine motor skills required to use them safely (Idle 1991).

The construction center also served as a great way to involve parents. Since we began engineering and design projects, parents who initially came in only for scheduled meetings were now visiting the classroom weekly to see their children's constructions. As their children led them to their creations, I realized that the students had told their parents a great deal about their work and this energy was spreading.

Let's Get to Work

On the day after the sledding party, the children rummaged through the stocking shelves of the classroom construction center to gather materials to make miniature sleds. After examining the materials, they sat down with their partners and drew a blueprint of their design (see Figure 1). Students understood blueprints as "a plan to help make something." They had learned to work with blueprints earlier in the year using Sammy's Science House CD-ROM from Edmark (1996), in which users choose a blueprint and click on materials to place, and Tigger's Contraptions CD-ROM from Disney (1997), in which users pick out images of recycled materials and assemble them with a mouse.

The children began to build their sleds on the third day in our classroom's construction center. They worked on their sleds every day during free time for two weeks. With adult supervision, some groups used a junior hacksaw to cut some pieces of wood and one group used a junior hand drill—all of these tools were manual tools, not power—to make holes to insert miniature flagpoles. Most groups used duct tape and masking tape for the sleds' final touches.

While I walked around the room to listen to their discussions, I noticed one group wanted to build its sled in the form of a triangle because both students liked the shape. They did not yet realize that the shape itself is a hindrance for sliding. I asked the group and surrounding students, "Do you think the shape of your sled will help it move smooth-ly through the snow?" and "Do you have an idea of how to build the skis so the shape does not matter?" Some children interjected that the points of the triangle would get caught unless they used some type of ski system. Other students suggested bending the cardboard to make the sled go down the hill more easily. Otherwise the points would get caught in the snow.

"Kid Watching"

I am always amazed at the unexpected ways in which children add to and improve their blueprints. During this stage of the creation process, I rarely interfere with the students' designs so as to avoid directing them to one right solution. Instead, I aim to develop the child's thinking, reasoning, and problem-solving skills, which has taught me to give up on the quiet classroom. This is a time for the children to talk, share, disagree, and create opportunities to learn. Be prepared for a high level of noise with this type of interaction.

I used my kid-watching skills to assess learning. Kid watching occurs when I stand back in the classroom and observe the children from a distance. I watch and listen to how they interact with each other, how they share tools, use their manners, and how they accept challenges. I also ask searching questions. These types of questions usually develop when I have the patience and courage to stand back and give them the time necessary to accomplish their goals. Children enjoy having opportunities to figure things out on their own and with the help of peers. As a teacher, the two questions I ask most are "How did you get that?" and "Why did you do it that way?" For this particular activity, most of the children's responses to my questions came from their past experiences, such as what they had observed with sleds and snowmobiles.

Sharing Knowledge

On the fourth day, the children stood in front of their kindergarten classmates and explained how their sleds were designed and built and how they thought their sleds would work in the snow. Some groups explained how they chose a design just by the looks and the color. Other students thought the whole concept out right down to the handle with which to carry the sled up the hill.

During the presentations, some groups' comments about their sleds included

- "We used a plastic-foam egg carton because it had 12 seats (holes) and our friends could sled together. The clothespins help keep the people in, and they act as a bumper in case we get close to the trees. Our skis are wood. We made a long handle so we could drag it up the hill for another ride"; and

- "We used cardboard because when Joe goes sledding he uses cardboard boxes and they go fast. We added a steering wheel so we can steer away from other sleds and trees. Our sled is covered so we do not get wet when it is snowing hard—it hurts my face when it snows really hard."

In their presentations, the children used engineering terminology correctly. I taught them earlier in the year that using engineering words would help them understand one another's ideas more clearly. In the sled presentations, for example, instead of saying "our sled needs to be bigger," they used the words *taller*, *wider*, and *heavier*. Those words helped with planning and building the sleds.

The sled-building activity allowed the children to use all the information learned in previous design projects about levers, linkages, and pulleys. In previous lessons, they used a pulley system to build a spider that could move up a web, a lever to create a turtle whose head moved in and out of its shell, and a gear system to make a simple clock.

One group, for example, incorporating what they had learned about pulleys, attached a string to their sled with a weight at the end. They tested it by placing the sled at the top of the classroom's indoor slide and letting the weight go. The sled worked on the smooth surface of the slide but did not function outdoors because of the snow. Another group knew from a previous lesson how to use a compass to draw a circle and then cut out a cone. They used this knowledge to make cones on their sleds to "guard your face from the snow."

Testing Celebration

The fifth day was a day of celebration. The children couldn't wait to test their designs out in the snow. Many of the children's parents came to school that day to see the sleds.

The students used weights ranging from 0.45 kg to 2.25 kg to put on the sleds. We made the weights by filling plastic bags with small pebbles until each weight increment was reached. Because the children's definition of a good sled was speed, all the sleds worked in some way. Their idea about a good sled changed, however, as they realized that just getting the sled down the hill presented a challenge. The sleds made of cardboard proved the fastest. I asked their creators, "Why is it so fast?" They figured it had to do with the curve of the cardboard.

The sleds with skis made it halfway down the hill but then stopped when they reached the bottom. Two sleds did not work at all because the weights kept sliding off. The children soon realized that they forgot to secure the weights to the sleds—the plastic bag containing the pebbles became very brittle and slippery outside.

The children's reactions to their sleds were mixed—some felt disappointed that their sleds did not make it off the top of the hill, some cheered as the sleds completed the run, and others wanted to go to a taller hill to see if height made a difference.

After testing the sleds for about 20 minutes, we went inside to discuss what worked well and what we could change. From their previous design activities, students had already realized that their creations don't always work the first time; sometimes we need to go back to tinker with a project to make it better.

Engineering Pluses

According to *Still More Activities That Teach* by Tom Jackson (2000), "for children entering the first grade in 1997, 50 percent of the jobs that they will have in their lifetime have not yet been invented." So how do you prepare children for those jobs? Jackson stresses the three Ts: technology, thinking skills, and team cooperation. I believe these life skills can be developed through engineering and design projects. The main goal in my projects is exposure—I want kindergarten students to begin exploring, problem solving, drawing blueprints, practicing tool safety, and working together with partners in cooperative learning groups.

Kindergarten children already believe that learning is fun, easy, and exciting. They also feel that they can do anything. These hands-on, action-oriented problem solvers are walking, talking engineers just ready to explore, build, and discover. Our job as teachers is to keep their playful attitude alive. Kindergarten rooms incorporate time for play; as children get older, this time quickly vanishes. As teachers we strive to keep this enjoyment and excitement for learning alive; engineering and design technology activities can help you do this. It has worked in our room—give it a try.

Gina A. Sarow teaches kindergarten at Unity Elementary School in Balsam Lake, Wisconsin.

References

Costa, A., and R. Liebmann. 1997. *Envisioning process as content: toward a renaissance curriculum.* Thousand Oaks, CA: Corwin.

Dunn, S., and R. Larson. 1990. *Design technology: Children's engineering.* Bristol, PA: The Flamer Press.

Idle, I. 1991. *Hands-on technology.* Cheltenham, England: Stanley Thornes.

Jackson, T. 2000. *Still more activities that teach.* Salt Lake City, UT: Red Rock.

Sigmon, J. F. 1997. Children's engineering: The use of design briefs. *The Technology Teacher* (56): 14–24.

Children's Literature

Iwamura, K. 1991. *The 14 forest mice and the winter sledding day.* Milwaukee, WI: Gareth Stevens.

Software

Ready for MATH with Pooh: Tigger's Contraptions. 1997. Burbank, CA: Disney Interactive.

Sammy's Science House: The Workshop. 1996. Redmond, WA: Edmark.

Connecting to the Standards

This article relates to the following National Science Education Standards (NRC 1996):

Teaching Standards

Standard A:
Teachers of science plan an inquiry-based science program for their students.

Standard B:
Teachers of science guide and facilitate learning and support inquiries while interacting with students.

Standard C:
Teachers guide students in self assessment.

Standard D:
Teachers structure the time available so that students are able to engage in extended investigations and create settings for student work that are flexible.

Content Standards

Standard A :
All K–4 students should develop an understanding of their abilities necessary to do scientific inquiry and understand scientific inquiry.

Standard B:
Objects should be made of one or more materials, such as paper, wood, and metal.

Standard E:
Students should be able to identify and implement a proposed solution, communicate a problem, and design a solution.

Journey Into the Five Senses

A rather ordinary topic can become a dynamic and meaningful inquiry.

Susan McWilliams

I admit to silently groaning when the teacher who agreed to participate in my study informed me that her class was embarking on a five senses project. I quickly discovered that my attitude was completely unfounded. At the time, I was a doctoral student at the University of Colorado at Denver researching inquiry teaching and learning. Neither my graduate coursework nor my experiences as a primary grade teacher prepared me for the variety of participants who collaborated with the teacher and her K–12 students during their four-week-long inquiry journeys into the five senses.

I'd like to share this inspiring project with you.

A Collaborative School Culture

By involving various school colleagues, a parent, a community member, and a museum, the teacher facilitated a collaborative approach to learning in her classroom.

From the outset, the teacher demonstrated that authentic science inquiry began with students. A few days before I first visited the classroom, the teacher read students a book about Helen Keller. The children were intrigued by Keller's experiences and began wondering about how the eyes and ears functioned. It was this curiosity that led the teacher to conduct the inquiry-based project on the five senses.

The development of conceptual understanding of the senses was not linear in this classroom. The project began with a study of the eyes, progressed toward the senses of touch and hearing, moved back to the eyes, addressed smelling and tasting, and then examined hearing again.

Throughout the study, children were provided with opportunities for further sense explorations during choice time—in this class it was during students' morning arrival time. During choice time, the teacher set up open-ended activities to promote thoughtful explorations, investigation, and

Inspiration for Inquiry

Their project began with an exploration of eyes. The teacher asked students to discuss what they knew about eyes. Some of the children's statements included:

- "I know the color of my eyes. They are hazel."
- "Without eyes, you wouldn't know where you were going."
- "There's a black dot in the middle."
- "Even though eyes are important, you can still live without them."
- "Eyes are squishy."
- "Your other senses work better when you're blind."
- "Eyes are fragile."

Initially, students posed only one question on the class chart paper: "Where is the cornea?," which was important to a student whose relative had a recent corneal transplant. As the discussion continued, however, students added two more questions:

- "What makes the color of the eye?"
- "What are the pupils for?"

The teacher explained that they would find answers to these questions over the next few weeks as they learned more about the eye and the other senses.

Topic: Senses
at www.scilinks.org
Enter code: SC020304

dialogue among students. Students chose the activity they were interested in and participated in it for as long as they liked during that time.

The Eyes Have It

After the introductory discussion, students used mirrors of different sizes—floor and handheld—to observe their own and their peers' eyes. Being careful not to touch any real eyes, children squinted at themselves in mirrors, opened their eyes as wide as possible, covered one eye and then the other with their hands, and closed both eyes then opened them slowly and quickly.

After about five minutes of exploration, the teacher encouraged students to concentrate on making "accurate" scientific observations "as real scientists do." Students observed their eyes for about 10 more minutes and then illustrated or wrote about their findings.

Finally, students came together "as real scientists do" to discuss what they observed. Their comments included:

- "There's a hole."
- "That's where tears come out of and your eyes start watering."
- "Your eye has different colors. You have different colored veins."
- "Winking is with one eye. Blinking is with two eyes."
- "You have lashes on the eyes on the bottom and the top."
- "When you move your head, your eyes move."
- "People have red in the bottom (of their eyes)."

At the end of their meeting, the teacher commended students on their interesting observations about the eyes and encouraged them to add any questions to the class chart to be explored later.

Listening and Creating

Students learned about the sense of hearing through a collaborative school effort. The teacher and the principal conducted a language lab in the principal's office with half the class at a time. The principal regularly schedules small groups of students in her office to support teachers and students in writing. The teacher read *The Listening Walk* (see "Children's Trade Books About the Five Senses"). Afterward, the group discussed the content and prepared to take their own listening walks outdoors.

The principal told the students, "One of my favorite things to listen to is the crackling of leaves. I wonder if I will hear the crackling of leaves on our listening walk."

The group took a listening walk outdoors, and when they returned the teacher asked students to write down or illustrate their observations. During this time, the children discussed what they heard on their walk:

- "I heard a squirrel climbing up the tree."
- "I heard the construction site building a house."
- "I heard construction and a squirrel climbing."
- "I heard birds 'tweet tweet' and leaves 'swish swash.'"

As the students talked about their experiences the principal said, "I notice that many of you are writing and spelling the word *heard*. It's got *ear* in the middle. Isn't that fun to look for? 'H 'ear' d.'"

The Doctor Is In

To explore the sense of smell, the teacher asked a student's parent who was a medical doctor to visit the classroom and lead in-depth sensory explorations about smell. To begin the visit, Dr. Dan drew a really big profile of a nose on chart paper to which children reacted with a collective "whoa." He discussed the various parts of the nose and their functions and then labeled his drawing.

Next, students conducted smelling investigations with Dr. Dan and the teacher. In this exploration, students tried to identify the scents of cotton balls placed in plastic cups and saturated with different scents, such as almond, lemon, alcohol, banana, peppermint, vinegar, and orange. Students recorded their observations as they investigated the scents.

Afterward, they met as a group to share and discuss what they observed. Dr. Dan asked, "What did we learn?" One child quickly responded, "We learned that our nose can tell what lemon is and what peppermint is." Dr. Dan agreed, and then directed students' attention to the large nose diagram they had drawn earlier to talk with students about how the nose actually works. Since many students were interested in "nasal secretions," Dr. Dan also discussed that nasal secretions help the nose to stay clean by keeping bacteria out.

Dr. Dan visited the classroom several more times during the sense study—to help students learn about hearing and tasting. When he returned to school to teach about hearing, Dr. Dan illustrated a large ear and its main components. Using a keyboard he brought with him, he told students about how the ear hears and demonstrated pitch and loudness variations.

In the taste session, students were asked to differentiate salt from sugar by sight, touch, and taste to solve the problem accurately. The tasting experience led to an in-depth study of the tongue with Dr. Dan.

Students were asked to notice where on the tongue they tasted the sugar and the salt. Near the end of the session, a student asked, "What does the rest of the tongue taste? The teacher pulled out a book on tasting and the tongue and opened it to a diagram showing the parts of the tongue. Together they learned that four main tastes—sweetness, sourness, saltiness, and bitterness—are discerned by taste buds located in specific areas on the tongue. Students used nonfiction books about tasting (see "Children's Trade Books About the Five Senses") to find out more about the sense of taste.

As they had done with their eyes, students also used mirrors to observe their tongues up close. Students observed their tongues for about 10 minutes and shared their observations as a class. Later, students created a large model of a tongue with foam board, bubble wrap (for the taste buds), paint, labels, and pushpins.

Revisiting Eyesight

To answer students' questions about the eye posed at the start of the project, the teacher invited a local ophthalmologist to the classroom. He brought a model of an eye, 12 cm in diameter, to introduce the different parts of the eye and discuss how the eye works. During his visit, Dr. Larry answered children's questions about eyes, including those from the chart paper and new ones that came up during the visit.

The next day, during Language Lab, the teacher taught students about the structure of a letter and reviewed the previous day's visit with Dr. Larry. The teacher recorded students' statements about what Dr. Larry taught them and ended the letter lesson by making a list of the vocabulary words: *pupil*, *cornea*, *iris*, *retina*, *optic nerve*, and *eye* and asking students to write or illustrate a thank-you note to Dr. Larry.

The following list is one group's reflection on what Dr. Larry taught them:

- "The eye is important."
- "Pupils are holes."
- "Eyes have six muscles. Two move the eye up and down, two move side to side, and two in the corners."
- "The cornea is the clear part over the eye. The pupil is in the middle. The iris is the color part."

When students finished their letters, they met as a group for sharing. Some students chose to read their letters to their classmates.

When he left, Dr. Larry lent the teacher the model of the eye for students' further explorations and reference. The children often referred to the model when they and their teacher read nonfiction literature about the eye.

Touch This

The sense of touch was predominantly addressed during choice time. One morning, students made a collage using various media of differing textures. Students chose from wire, velvet, sandpaper, corrugated cardboard, sponges, steel wool, fake fur, and many other media. While working, students talked with each other informally about what the textures reminded them of in their experiences and were prompted with questions from the teacher, such as "How does that feel?" "Is this smooth or rough?"

To further explore the sense of touch, the students and the teacher created two feeling boxes during choice time. Feeling boxes were boxes with a hole cut just large enough for a hand, but not large enough that the contents of the box were visible. Students decorated the boxes, and, each day, the teacher changed the object in the boxes. Many times the feeling boxes became the first focus of attention in the morning.

To the Museum

To cap off the project, the teacher planned a trip to the Denver Museum of Nature and Science. Students were divided into two groups and attended informational sessions presented by the Hall of Life Health Education Center. K–1 students learned about how the ears and eyes function by watching a demonstration with large take-apart ear and eye models, examined a Braille book, observed sound waves made with a tuning fork placed in water, tested their taste buds, and performed various smell and touch experiments.

The second-grade students observed the dissection of a cow's eye, experienced demonstrations of sound waves, and participated in an examination of the three tiny bones in the ear. All of the students were captivated during the field trip and returned with information to share.

A Sense of Reflection

This project demonstrated how a rather ordinary topic—the study of the five senses—can become a dynamic and meaningful inquiry when a teacher takes steps to extend learning beyond the school to the community and its resources.

During this five senses project, the teacher nurtured her students' curiosity through several means: revisiting facets of the topic in further depth; providing opportunities for children to choose explorations and investigations related to the study; giving children the support to ask questions and find out information; and maintaining resources such as nonfiction literature, tools, and models.

The teacher believed that building a collaborative partnership with members in the community would help her students become completely involved with the topic of study—and it did. When I interviewed students for preassessment at the beginning of the unit, only two could list the five senses accurately. By the end of the project, the students not only told me what the five senses were but also elaborated with interesting facts.

Including experts and field trips in the project helped students begin to see that numerous sources and experiences are required for learning about a topic of study. In this project, the teacher not only fostered inquiry learning but also modeled authentic professional collaboration and strengthened a community partnership composed of educators, professionals, parents, and learners.

Susan McWilliams (susan_mcwilliams@sdstate. edu) *is an assistant professor of early childhood education at South Dakota State University in Brookings, South Dakota. Because this project was part of educational research conducted at the University of Denver in Colorado, the teacher's name and school location was not revealed.*

Resources

Gallas, K. 1995. *Talking their way into science: Hearing children's questions and theories, responding with curricula.* New York: Teachers College.

Heuser, D. 2002. *Reworking the workshop: Math and science reform in the primary grades.* Portsmouth, NH: Heinemann.

National Research Council (NRC). 1996. *National Science Education Standards.* Washington, DC: National Academy Press.

Saul, W., J. Reardon, C. Pearce, D. Dieckman, and D. Neutze. 2002. *Science workshop: Reading, writing, and thinking like a scientist.* 2nd ed. Portsmouth, NH: Heinemann.

Saul, W., J. Reardon, A. Schmidt, C. Pearce, D. Blackwood, and M. Bird. 1993. *Science workshop: A whole language approach.* Portsmouth, NH: Heinemann.

Children's Trade Books About the Five Senses

Baker, P. 1998. *My first book of sign.* Washington, DC: Kendall Green.

Bennett, P. 1998. *My brain and senses.* Parsippany, NJ: Silver Press.

Browne, A. 1998. *Voices in the park.* New York: DK Publishing.

Bryan, J. 1993. *Sound and vision.* New York: Dillon.

Cole, J. 1999. *The magic school bus explores the five senses.* New York: Scholastic.

Collins, H. 1995. *Songs in sign.* Eugene, OR: Garlic Press.

Hurwitz, S. 1998. *Hearing.* New York: Franklin Watts.

Hurwitz, S. 1998. *Sight.* New York: Franklin Watts.

Hurwitz, S. 1998. *Smell.* New York: Franklin Watts.

Hurwitz, S. 1998. *Taste.* New York: Franklin Watts.

Hurwitz, S. 1998. *Touch.* New York: Franklin Watts.

Jackson, M. 1995. *My five senses.* Austin, TX: Steck-Vaughn.

Lundell, M. 1995. *A girl named Helen Keller.* New York: Scholastic.

Miller, M. 1994. *My five senses.* New York: Alladdin.

Savran, S. 1997. *The human body.* Chicago: Kidsbooks.

Showers, P. 1991. *The listening walk.* New York: Harper Collins.

Tatchell, J. 1997. *How do your senses work?* London: Usborne.

Connecting to the Standards

This article relates to the following National Science Education Standards (NRC 1996):

Grades K–4

Content Standards:

Standard A: Science as Inquiry

- Abilities to do scientific inquiry
- Understanding about scientific inquiry

Standard C: Life Science

- The characteristics of organisms

Standard F: Science in Personal and Social Perspectives

- Personal health

Assessing Understanding

Drawing on Student Understanding

Through artistic experiences, students experience science as a human endeavor that uses the full range of human creativity.

Mary Stein, Shannan McNair, and Jan Butcher

Visitors are delighted and amazed when they come upon beautifully detailed drawings of a wide variety of insects in the halls of Upland Hills School. More intriguing is that these beautiful drawings were created by students ages 7–12. At the Lowry Center for Early Childhood Education, drawings of turtles with patterned shells adorn the kindergarten classroom walls. In the preschool classroom, drawings of ducks hatching from eggs are displayed along one wall and bees of various sizes line the hallway.

Drawing has always helped artists closely observe and reflect on their ideas; however, using drawing as a tool to help students develop and document more complex understandings is not often used in science instruction. Here we discuss reasons for using art as a tool for deepening scientific concept knowledge and some essential components for creating a successful learning experience.

The Art and Science Connection

Art and science often have been viewed as very different—even opposing—disciplines with art being viewed as creative expression and science being portrayed as a fact-based discipline with a lockstep approach to solving problems. This view of science does not accurately portray the creativity inherent in science, nor does it serve to help students think about science as a human endeavor (Stein and Power 1996).

The National Science Education Standards (NRC 1996) emphasize science as inquiry. The Standards also highlight science as a human endeavor and suggest ways that emphases in science teaching change as the Standards are implemented. Using artistic expression as a tool for learning supports the Standards by enhancing students' abilities to communicate science explanations, engage in science as a means for explanation, and communicate their ideas to the public and to their classmates (NRC 1996).

Integrating Drawing With Learning About Animals

As part of a semester-long science class, co-author Jan Butcher's students were engaged in an in-depth study of animals. The students ranged in age from 7–12 years, so she was careful to create learning experiences in which students had opportunities to further their understandings independent of developmental levels. One component of the class included the study of insects. Students found insects in their natural habitats, studied insects from an assortment of books and field guides, observed live catches (which were later returned to their environment) in glass jars, and examined parts of insects with magnifying lenses and microscopes. The instructional activities also included readings and discussions about insect classification, life cycles, and identification.

As one part of the study, students chose an insect about which they wanted to learn. They used resources such as books (see "Student Resources"), living insects that had been collected, specimens from a mounted insect collection, and posters and photographs to create detailed drawings of the insects. The students became completely engaged in the assignment, and the detail and quality of their drawings were astounding (Figure 1). When questioned about the process, one student's comments provided insight into how drawing can help deepen understanding: "It is like when you draw it, it becomes your

Topic: Explore insects
at *www.scilinks.org*
Enter code: SC0101

Figure 1. Children of all ages were able to participate in the project. These drawings (figures 1 through 4) represent samples from stu-dents ranging in age from 7 to 12.

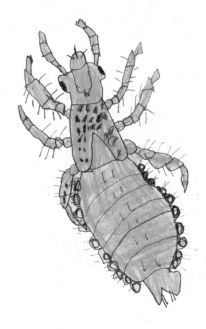

own. You pay attention and draw the things you are interested in."

At the Lowry Center, preschool and kindergarten children pursue project work to learn about animals. Through a variety of experiences, they gain a greater awareness of animal names, appearances, movements, sounds, and diet. Each of the children's drawings is different, because the drawings are representations of a student's individual experience and understandings of the animals. As students learn more about animals, their drawings reflect their increased knowledge and interest in particular animals. The following approaches help to successfully integrate drawing with science learning:

Safety With Insects and Animals

When handling insects and animals it is very important that the teacher use safe, humane procedures. This usually requires that the teacher have access to specific information about the animals or insects that the children will be observing. The teacher should include rules and procedures for students to follow when studying animals. For example, students should wear gloves when handling specimens and should be careful not to harm the insect or animal. Specific information about the use and care of animals in the classroom can be found at the NSTA websites: *199.0.3.5/handbook/animals.asp* and *199.0.3.5/handbook/organisms.asp.*

Children learn to look for insects outdoors during the cool mornings, when the cold-blooded creatures are moving more slowly. Stinging insects are either observed from some distance or dead specimens are gathered and placed in magnifying boxes for closer examination. Children are told not to handle spiders until an adult has identified them as harmless. Gathering insects is done with a plastic cup and a large index card—the children scoop up the insect carefully with a cup and slide the index card underneath. Insects are observed for the day and then released outdoors.

- promoting student ownership
- connecting drawing to specific science learning experiences,
- providing resources, and
- providing teacher modeling.

Student Ownership

Individual students have special interests and are more likely to be engaged when they make choices to direct the learning activity. The Upland Hills students were given the opportunity to learn about and observe various insects through experiences such as field observations and exposure to literature and media before they selected which insect they would like to draw in detail.

Unlike some classroom activities in which all students are creating the same artifact, this activity was based on student interest, and the drawings and the ways students chose to represent their insects varied. Competition among students was reduced because they were creating a unique drawing—they were not worried that a fellow student could draw a particular insect better

than they could. With this variety, characteristics could be compared and contrasted.

Another component of student ownership involved students' natural interest in drawing as a means to communicate—most students love to draw. When the students were told their drawings would be displayed in the hall outside the classroom, their enthusiasm was clear. They worked hard, paid attention to detail, and had fun in the process (Figure 2).

Children at the Lowry Center are encouraged to draw many things throughout the day, and a variety of materials—markers, colored pencils, paints, and crayons, and an assortment of paper—are always available for them to use. For example, they might be asked to draw their plan for the day, what they observed on a walk, an illustration of a mathematics solution, or a pictorial version of a recipe or rules to a game.

When children become excited about something they are exploring, they have a natural desire to represent that experience. For example, when a teacher brought baby

Figure 2. It was clear from the students' drawings that they paid attention to the details of the insect they chose to draw.

ducklings into the kindergarten classroom, one boy immediately got a piece of paper and pencil and began drawing the ducklings. Their drawings are an important part of class-created newsletters that give parents information about the children's experiences during the week. Children recall what they learned and what they liked and then illustrate this within the newsletter. Students also use journals to record their experiences.

Connecting Drawing to Science

These students had spent a significant amount of time learning about insects through teacher-guided experiences. They found insects in their natural habitats, recorded their observations in the field and then shared their findings with other students in class discussions.

Through reading, observation, and class discussion, students learned about insect types and characteristics, habitats, and interesting facts. They also learned about the important role insects play in our world. When students were asked to select an insect to draw, their learning experiences had not only prepared them for the activity but also had made them eager to begin. Drawing an insect was a creative way in which students could communicate their detailed understandings. Before beginning to draw, students were asked to identify the body parts they had learned about. They were also asked to think about their drawing as a way to show all the details modeled by Nancy Winslow Parker and Joan Richards Wright in *Bugs* (1987).

The objective of the activity was to reinforce students' learning and aid younger students who knew the body parts but could not name them: *head, thorax, abdomen, six legs* (Figure 3). The experience also provided a direct learning experience: Students used their fingers, hands, and eyes to link their reading and listen to their own observations. For example, often a student had ideas about how to draw a particular insect based on field observations, but then had a desire to use additional references to check the details of his or her ideas.

Following special classroom presentations that exposed students to something new, children at the Lowry Center often used drawing to capture those experiences. After a presentation on rain forest animals—in which zoological professionals brought rain forest animals (macaw, clouded leopard, boa constrictor, gecko, frogs, and a sloth) into the

Figure 3. These drawings show how students included one of the lesson objectives—to learn insect body parts—within their drawings.

classroom—children in the classroom drew detailed pictures of the sloth. The amount of interest in that particular animal was probably due to the fact that sloths look very different from more familiar animals and because none of the children had ever seen a sloth.

Following a special presentation by an entomologist, a student drew a praying mantis. Other children drew shiny beetles with impressive pincers, while some drew dragonflies or butterflies with colorful wings. Similarly, after outdoor hikes, children used drawings to represent and revisit their experiences. After a hike to a pond, one student drew the goose she had seen. Other children drew minnows and water spiders, representing what they could see around and on the surface of the water. Students drew what is underneath the surface when an aquarium

was filled with water and life from a pond for classroom observation. A piece of butcher paper taped to the table holding the aquarium made a nice tablet for ongoing drawings of the children's observations.

Young children can often express their understanding and concept development more effectively through drawings than verbally or in written assignments. They are often more engaged in details of their understanding when they draw. Examining drawings, their emerging understandings become evident. For example, many young children will place a humanlike face on their animals (Figure 4) that is eventually

Figure 4. Young children often draw human characteristics such as a face with a smile on their animals. As their understanding develops, so do their drawings.

They have 6 legs.
They all have 7 spots—
(my babysitter told me).
They have antennaes to feel & hea

replaced by a more accurate representation. When students draw both before and after an experience, the drawings can serve as an assessment tool for the teacher. For example, in a second drawing of the same insect, one student adds more detail, along with the features of wings, head, and antennae. He also shows much greater detail of the bee's stinger after he has learned about bees in the class. Other characteristics, such as the relative length of frog and turtle legs and the details of caterpillar legs, are reflected in children's representations of their animals.

Providing Resources

It is one thing to make close observations in the field and something quite different to record your observations on paper. The drawing and writing process, in itself, encourages students to think more deeply about what they believe. It can be a way for them to continue to explore an idea or concept. Many questions begin to emerge: How many legs did it have? How many body sections? Were the legs hairy? Did the insect have antennae? What did the insect's eyes look like?

Students need various resources to help them answer the questions that emerge. In addition to live animals and insects, students had other resources that helped them find their own answers to their inquiries. Representing something that has been observed involves recalling significant details, thinking about the relative size of body parts and background in the picture, and choosing colors or making patterns that match the model. They also used scientific tools such as hand lenses and books with photographs to help them with their work (see "Resources").

Teacher Modeling

At the Lowry Center teachers modeled careful observation of detail when hiking or conducting classroom explorations. They also modeled sketching things they wanted to remember, using a nature log on hikes or a child's block construction to show a parent.

When students were drawing their insects in the classroom, the teacher also modeled the process. She was as busy as the students in learning about her insect of choice, drawing her insect using the same information, processes, and resources that students used. The teacher's role became one of modeling through example. When students observe their teacher engaged in the same activity as they are, it helps assure them that the activity is important and worthwhile and, at the same time, shows them the activity is a learning experience for the teacher.

Deeper Learning

These examples show how art and drawing can be used as a tool to deepen student understanding. Just as an emphasis on writing to learn has emerged as a means to deepen understanding, drawing is another tool through which students can be encouraged to think deeply about what they know and have observed. Student questioning that arises during this process also suggests that drawing can be used to encourage inquiry. It is important to view the drawing activity as a student-centered inquiry through which students can express their creativity and find answers to their own questions; otherwise, integrating drawing may be no more useful than having students copy sentences out of a book.

People often compartmentalize their knowledge and strengths by saying things like "I'm a math and science person" or "My strength is in language and the arts." As educators we recognize these labels and narrow definitions can serve to limit what our students believe they are good at and eventually what they will choose to do. Broadening students' perspectives by integrating art as a tool for scientific inquiry enables students to become more reflective and aware of their understanding.

As questions emerge, students learn how to find answers to these questions and how their artistic creations can be used to communicate what they have learned. Through artistic experiences, students experience science as a human endeavor that uses the full range of human creativity and does not promote science and art as opposite ends of a continuum. As students begin to view themselves as artists, scientists, and humans unhampered by labels, all of society will reap the benefits of artistic expressions.

Mary Stein is an assistant professor in the Department of Curriculum, Instruction, and Leadership at Oakland University in Rochester, Michigan, and president of the Council for Elementary Science International (CESI); Shannan McNair is an assistant professor of Early Childhood Education at Oakland University in Rochester, Michigan; and Jan Butcher is an elementary teacher with a special interest in science at Upland Hills School in Oxford, Michigan.

The authors thank the students at Upland Hills School and the Lowry Early Childhood Center for Early childhood Education for sharing their work.

Resources

Doris, E. 1991. *Doing what scientists do: Children learn to investigate their world.* Portsmouth, NH: Heinemann.

Hein, G., and S. Price. 1994. *Active assessment for active science: A guide for elementary school teachers.* Portsmouth, NH: Heinemann.

Humphryes, J. 2000. Exploring nature with children. *Young Children* 55 (2): 16–20.

National Research Council (NRC). 1996. *National Science Education Standards.* Washington, DC: National Academy Press.

Ross, M. E. 2000. Science their way. *Young Children* 55 (2): 6–13.

Stein, M.T., and B. A. Power. 1996. Putting art on the scientist's palette. In eds. R. S. Hubbard and K. Ernst, *New Entries: Learning by writing and drawing.* Portsmouth, NH: Heinemann.

Student Resources

Blum, M. 1998. *Bugs in 3-D.* San Francisco: Chronicle.

Lavies, B. 1990. *Backyard hunter: The praying mantis.* New York: Dutton.

Mound, L. 1993. *Eyewitness junior amazing insects.* New York: Knopf.

Parker, N. W., and J. R. Wright. 1987. *Bugs.* New York: Greenwillow.

Ryder, J. 1989. *Where butterflies grow.* New York: Lodestar.

Still, J. 1991. *Amazing beetles: Eyewitness juniors.* New York: Knopf.

Suzuki, D., and B. Hehner. 1991. *Looking at insects.* New York: John Wiley.

Also in Science and Children

Glanville, L. 1998. Bug buddies. *Science and Children* 35 (7): 22–25.

Palopoli, M. L. 1998. The mantis project. *Science and Children* 35 (2): 34–39, 54.

The Tree of Life

Students began to make connections between humans and their actions and the rain forest and other environments.

Donna M. Plummer, Jeannie MacShara, and Skila King Brown

With only so many hours of instructional time in the day and so much content to be covered in different academic areas, interdisciplinary lessons are, for many teachers, a necessary component of the elementary classroom curriculum.

One way teachers can make connections between subjects is by using children's literature. Incorporating literature into other academic areas—especially science—can create a bridge between subjects and reinforce scientific concepts while providing additional opportunities for reading and writing. It's a time-efficient strategy that meshes well with the thematic approach to learning used in many elementary classrooms and helps students connect what they are learning throughout the day.

With these thoughts in mind, we—a college science methods professor, a student teacher, and a K–1 classroom teacher— teamed up to create an exciting interdisciplinary lesson for young children based on the book *Tree of Life: The World of the Af-*

rican Baobab (Bash 1989). The lesson helped introduce such concepts as life cycles and the interdependence of plants and animals and provided children with a basis for connections to later classroom learning. My role in the lesson was to facilitate the teachers' planning and to observe the lesson taught by the student teacher.

A Web for Learning

The teachers chose to use *Tree of Life* because the supervising teacher was familiar with the book and because the class, which followed a thematic approach to curriculum, was studying plants, animals, and the environment. The book, with its main theme of interdependence, linked the three topics perfectly.

The teachers' initial preparation for the lesson began by brainstorming a "thematic web" for the book to highlight connections across the curriculum (see Figure 1). Their web included a variety of experiences and integrated subject matter knowledge in the different areas of the curriculum, including science, social studies, vocabulary, and art.

Although not all the ideas identified on their thematic web ended up being covered in the lesson, the web was a useful planning tool that can be modified as themes are taught from year to year.

By the end of their planning session, the teachers had come up with a plan of action and three lesson objectives for students:

- Recognize the stages of the life cycle of the tree and its interdependence with the various organisms.
- Write summaries of what each living thing needs from the tree.
- Create a replica of the tree and all its organisms.

Once the objectives were set, the teachers began gathering the necessary materials for the classroom experiences with the children. The student teacher constructed a "base" baobab tree using brown butcher paper obtained from the school library. The trunk was approximately one meter across with spreading roots. Seven brown butcher-paper branches were glued to the trunk. Construction paper of varying colors and painting supplies were gathered with which students could construct the different organisms represented in the book.

What's It All About?

When the preparations were completed, the teacher introduced the book to students. She discussed its title and its author as well as the cover artwork and illustrator. She then asked students to guess what they might learn from this book. She told students to think about what they already knew about trees and reminded them that it was possible they might hear some of that same information in this new book. This discussion gave the teacher an additional opportunity to review with students information learned previously about trees.

Most students guessed that the book was about a big tree, while others thought it might be about animals based on the elephants and birds represented on the cover. A few thought it might tell about a tree's life.

After the introduction, the teacher read the book aloud to the students. The book's rich artwork and intricate illustrations enthralled the students.

Afterwards, the class discussed the importance of the tree and how it is the center of its environment. The teacher talked about the interrelationships among the organisms associated with the baobab tree. For example, the baboons eat fresh fruit from the tree and the yellow-billed hornbill lays her eggs in a tree hollow. As they talked, students began to recognize the connections among living beings. They also began to understand the significance of the tree and how many organisms depend on it for survival.

The teacher reread the book, and the class listed all the living things mentioned in the book, such as chameleons, fruit bats, and hornbills.

The students then chose an organism from the book to draw. Each student chose a different organism to represent. About one hour was allowed for drawing an organism on construction or butcher paper. The students then painted the drawings with tempera paints. Several students created two organisms.

Our Tree

Now it was time for the students to complete the tree replica the student teacher had begun earlier. The tree was hung in a hallway so that everyone would be able to see the results. Students spent an additional hour working on the tree. They created leaves and petals from green and white construction papers and sponge-painted the tree bark, using black and gray tempera paint to create textured bark and simulate shadows. The students then taped their drawings of the tree's inhabitants on the appropriate areas of the tree. Discussion among students regarding the different organisms encouraged appropriate placement on the tree. The book was available as a reference for any student who was unsure of the correct placement.

Finally, students wrote, and later typed on the classroom computer, a short sentence about their organism to place on the display. They included observations such as "The fruit bat sips the pollen from the flower," "The giraffe uses its neck to eat the leaves," and "These animals depend on this tree."

The hallway display of student work also provided an additional benefit—it let students display and explain to others their knowledge gained from the book. Students could tell passersby the name of their organisms as well as the special relationship of their organisms to the tree.

Assessing Knowledge

For assessment, the teacher evaluated the sentences to see that each student understood the significance of the tree to his or her organism and worded it accordingly. For example, one student wrote, "The yellow-billed hornbill finds a hollowed place in the tree and lays her eggs." When probed, this student elaborated, "[It] depends on making its nest there. They hatch and break out in six weeks."

The teacher also monitored to see that each child knew the appropriate position for his or her organism on the tree. For example, students recognized that elephants are found living on the ground in the vicinity of the tree, while fruit bats can be found hanging from a branch of the tree.

Students were interviewed by the student teacher in groups of five to document further their understanding of these relationships. During the interviews, students read their sentences describing their animals to demonstrate their ability to communicate, a science process skill. The student teacher also prompted elaboration on the students' sentences during these brief interviews.

Primed for Further Learning

Students built on the knowledge gained from the *Tree of Life* interdisciplinary lessons. When the class began studying environments, the teacher again used a related science trade book to spur learning.

In *Rain Forest* by Helen Cowcher (1990), humans' impact on the organisms of the forest is visually and emotionally presented. After reading this book, students developed appropriate vocabulary and sketched and colored creatures of the rain forest—much like they had done after reading *Tree of Life*.

Because the students had been introduced previously to animals and plants through *Tree of Life* and other activities, they were better able to understand the concepts presented in the new book. Because they had studied the life cycle of the painted lady butterfly, students recognized the blue morpho butterfly in *Rain Forest* as similar to the butterflies they knew from their own environment.

Figure 1. Tree of Life Thematic Web.

Social Studies

Compare/contrast with/*Desert Giant* by Barbara Bash

Art

• Sponge-paint trunk of tree to match book's description

• Draw, color, cut figures

Science

• Interdependence
• Identify the animals/insects
• Categorize: herbivore/carnivore
• Diurnal/nocturnal
• Life cycle

Math

• Discuss sizes of animals
• Cut out organisms (elephants to insects) in realistic proportions

Reading

• Word Wall for vocabulary development

*describing words:

careless	slender
gnarled	leafless
crookedly	protective
tender	restless
lush	velvety
gaping	

*senses — phrases

Writing

• Write a summary statement about an animal in relation to the tree.

• On-demand task: Why do you think Aftican tribesment name each tree "um" (mother)?

• Which animal did you find most interesting? Why?

Throughout their lessons the teachers observed students' continuing development of concepts, such as interdependence. In particular, students began to make connections between humans and their actions and the rain forest and other environments.

Everyone Gains

Through these experiences with trade books and follow-up activities, students were not only introduced to a new environment but also were exposed to concepts they could apply to other environments, including their own. Students began to see how the information they were learning was connected—how living things depended on other living things. Another benefit resulting from this approach was the students' ability to relate one book to another. Often students could finish the sentence of one book based upon the knowledge they had gained from a previously read book.

This experience helped the student teacher discover the benefits of using a hands-on project to assess students. For the classroom teacher and myself, the lesson's success reinforced our belief in the benefits of thematic, cross-subject planning and teaching. I began to incorporate more interdisciplinary teaching strategies in my college education courses. Recently, I added a number of children's literature selections as required readings in my science methods class for elementary education majors.

Overall, using trade books to spur learning and creating thematic webs based on the books ensured that a variety of curriculum areas was incorporated into learning. In addition, it provided the opportunity for brainstorming among colleagues. We discovered many rewards of thematic teaching using trade books, encouraging its continued implementation in future lessons.

Donna M. Plummer is an assistant professor of education at Centre College, and Jeannie Mac-Shara is a primary literacy coach at Woodlawn Elementary, both in Danville, Kentucky. At the time of this project, Skila King Brown was a student teacher at Woodlawn Elementary School.

Resources

Bash, B. 1989. *Tree of life: The world of the African baobab.* Boston: Little, Brown.

Cowcher, H. 1990. *Rain forest.* New York: Farrar, Straus, and Giroux.

National Research Council (NRC). 1996. *National Science Education Standards.* Washington, DC: National Academy Press.

Peetoom, A. 1993. Prologue: Little children lead the way. In ed. S. Tehudi, *The Astonishing Curriculum: Integrating science and humanities through language,* 1–10. Urbana, IL: National Council of Teachers of English.

Connecting to the Standards

This article relates to the following National Science Education Standards (NRC 1996):

Grades K–4

Content Standards:

Standard A: Science as Inquiry
- Abilities to do scientific inquiry
- Understanding about scientific inquiry

Standard C: Life Science
- The characteristics of organisms

Standard F: Science in Personal and Social Perspectives
- Personal health

Students' Ideas About Plants

Even young students appeared to understand many basic characteristics of plants and their needs.

Charles R. Barman, Mary Stein, Natalie S. Barman, and Shannan McNair

Science and Children invited kindergarten to grade 8 teachers to participate in a study investigating students' ideas about plants and plant growth in the fall of 2001 (Barman et al. 2002). Two hundred twenty-seven individuals from 16 states in the United States, one U.S. Territory, and one Canadian Province responded to this invitation and contributed data from more than 2,400 students.

Rationale for Study

In previous work with students, a number of researchers (McNair and Stein 2001; Ryman 1974; Tunnicliffe and Reiss 2000; Osborne and Freyberg 1985; Stepens 1985; Bell 1981) have found that student understanding of plants and what plants need to grow is often limited. For example, in McNair and Stein's research (2001), when asked to draw a plant, both children and adults most often drew or thought about flowering plants. Bell (1981) found that some children did not consider trees to be plants. Researchers also found that students were more likely to consider

an organism to be a plant if it possessed specific characteristics or parts, such as flowers or stems (Ryman 1974).

When considering what plants need to grow, ideas can become even more complicated. According to the National Science Education Standards (NRC 1996), students in kindergarten to grade four should understand that plants have basic needs that include air, water, nutrients, and light. However, the idea that plants need things provided by people may make more sense to young students than plants' having basic needs. For example, we water our plants, set them in a lighted space, and plant them in soil. These needs may be more obvious to students than the idea that plants need air to grow.

In addition, students often ascribe human characteristics to organisms as they interpret the organism's attributes and functions with respect to their own experiences (Osborne and Freyberg 1985; Stein and McNair 2002). Students often believe that plants need food in a way that is similar to the way people do. So, when students hear that plants "make their own food," they are often thinking about food in terms of something that the plant ingests or eats or that plants obtain their food through their roots (Roth 1985; Smith and Anderson 1984; Barker 1995).

Because the National Science Education Standards outline specific things kindergarten to grade 8 students should know about plants (see "Connecting to the Standards") and previous data indicated that elementary students had difficulty understanding some major ideas about plants and plant growth, an investigation that would determine the current thinking of elementary and middle school students about these topics seemed appropriate. After all, plants are a vital component of our Earth, and they are the basic connection between the Sun and the energy flow that exists in all ecosystems.

Data Collection Procedures

The investigators who participated in this study followed an interview protocol that was included in the September 2002 *Science and Children* invitation. In this protocol, the investigators were provided with one set of pictures depicting plants and objects that are not plants and another set of pictures showing things plants need or don't need for growth.

Using the first set of pictures, the investigators asked each student to classify the pictures as *plants* or *not plants* and to explain what all plants have in common. With the second set of pictures, the students were asked to identify the things plants need for growth and to explain how each of the things they identified actually help a plant grow. (For a complete description of the interview protocol, refer to the September 2002 issue of *Science and Children* or view the article at *www.nsta.org/elementaryschool.*)

After the investigators completed collecting data from individual students, all of the students' responses were transferred to a group tally sheet and sent to a central location for compilation and analysis.

The Results: Which Items Were Plants?

Figure 1 shows the results of students' classification of items as plants or not plants. Overall, the kindergarten to grade 8 students surveyed had a consistent grasp of which pictures depicted plants and which did not. For example, most of the students were able to identify the picture of the flower as a plant, and there was consensus that the bush, Venus flytrap, and fern were plants.

Most students knew that bread mold wasn't a plant; however, about half misclassified the mushroom as a plant. This latter finding supports earlier research in which investigators found students were more likely to identify an organism as a plant as long as it had structures that looked plantlike (Ryman 1974). In this case, the stalk of the mushroom resembles the stem of a plant.

When reviewing the students' responses, it became evident that characteristics students strongly associate with plants are:
- They have leaves and stems;
- They are green; and
- They grow in the ground/soil.

Thus, students very frequently selected the flower, fern, and bush as being examples of plants, as these examples clearly show these characteristics. They were less sure of the grass, oak tree, pine tree, and Venus flytrap.

Some interesting differences were apparent in the way students at different grade levels identified plants. Students in grades 6

Figure 1. Students' Responses to "Is this a plant or not a plant?"

Interview Item	Grades K–2 (n = 869)			Grades 3–5 (n = 1019)			Grades 6–8 (n = 528)		
	Yes	No	Not Sure	Yes	No	Not Sure	Yes	No	Not Sure
Grass	81%	17%	2%	86%	12%	2%	78%	15%	7%
Flowering plant	97%	2%	1%	95%	4%	1%	96%	2%	2%
Oak tree	81%	16%	3%	88%	10%	2%	78%	16%	6%
Bush	87%	10%	3%	87%	12%	1%	86%	9%	5%
Seeds	55%	39%	6%	51%	38%	11%	37%	50%	13%
Mushroom	57%	38%	5%	60%	30%	10%	50%	37%	13%
Venus flytrap	73%	19%	8%	80%	14%	6%	74%	16%	10%
Walking stick (insect)	5%	92%	3%	9%	88%	3%	4%	93%	3%
Pine tree	84%	15%	1%	86%	11%	3%	77%	16%	7%
Fern	88%	10%	2%	90%	7%	3%	86%	9%	5%
Telephone pole	6%	93%	1%	3%	96%	1%	3%	95%	3%
Bread mold	8%	85%	7%	16%	74%	10%	12%	76%	12%

to 8 appeared to have more difficulty identifying certain organisms as plants than the students in kindergarten to grade 5. For example, 78% of the students in grades 6 to 8 identified grass as a plant, while 81% of the students in kindergarten to grade 2 and 86% of the students in grades 3 to 5 identified grass as a plant.

The same pattern was shown in how the students classified an oak tree and a pine tree. Although there are many possible explanations, one possibility is that students begin with a fairly narrow definition of a plant and subsequently broaden it as they are exposed to more examples in school and in their daily lives. Then, as students learn more about scientific classification schemes they begin to narrow these broadened definitions once again.

The two items that appeared most difficult for students to characterize were the seeds and the mushroom. This is not surprising because seeds have the potential to become a plant and mushrooms have many plantlike characteristics. These two items elicited many explanations from students, such as "plants come from seeds" and "plants are green," to let the teacher know why they were characterizing the picture as "yes," "no," or "not sure."

The Results: What Do Plants Need to Grow?

Figure 2 displays kindergarten to grade 8 students' ideas about what a plant needs for growth. Like the data related to identifying plants, the results are fairly consistent at all grade levels. For example, most students identified the Sun, water, potting soil, and air as the most important factors in plant growth.

When considering what plants need in order to grow, students tended to attribute anthropomorphic characteristics to plants. They discussed plants as needing what humans require in order to grow. The ideas that plants "eat," "drink," and "breathe" were expressed frequently. For example, when talking about the importance of water for plants, students generally felt water was needed for the plant to "drink" or provided nutrients for the plant.

Although *plant food* is a term commonly used to describe plant fertilizer, most students identified plant food as one of the most important factors in plant growth. One student stated: "Plant food keeps the plant from getting hungry." Although students often explained that plants "eat" when describing plant food, very few students at any grade level indicated that plants needed the "people food" (examples of cereal and sandwich). It appears that, while they think plants "eat," the students also have some understanding that plants eat different things and through different types of processes.

When talking about the Sun, the students in kindergarten to grade 2 generally said it helps the plant grow by "warming" the plant. The students in grades 3 to 8 said the Sun helps the plant make food, gives the plant energy, and provides heat for the plant. Even though these students stated that the Sun helps plants make food and gives plants energy, there was very little discussion about photosynthesis or the process of how plants make their own food. The students' discus-

Figure 2. Students' Responses to "Do plants need this to grow?"

	Grades K–2 (n = 869)			Grades 3–5 (n = 1019)			Grades 6–8 (n = 528)		
Interview Item	Yes	No	Not Sure	Yes	No	Not Sure	Yes	No	Not Sure
Sun	93%	6%	1%	98%	1%	1%	99%	1%	0%
Lightbulb	13%	84%	3%	14%	82%	4%	19%	79%	2%
Water	95%	5%	0%	98%	1%	1%	99%	1%	0%
Box of cereal	11%	88%	1%	1%	99%	0%	2%	94%	4%
Bee	44%	51%	5%	53%	40%	7%	44%	50%	6%
Plant food	86%	10%	4%	77%	18%	5%	69%	23%	8%
Worm	41%	55%	4%	46%	48%	6%	37%	54%	9%
Air	78%	19%	3%	81%	14%	5%	83%	13%	4%
Oxygen	58%	29%	13%	67%	25%	8%	64%	32%	4%
Carbon dioxide	30%	46%	24%	59%	28%	13%	65%	23%	12%
Sandwich	3%	95%	2%	1%	98%	1%	2%	94%	4%
Potting soil	88%	10%	2%	88%	9%	3%	83%	13%	4%

sion showed no apparent link between carbon dioxide and photosynthesis.

Young children seemed to understand that plants need water and sunlight. A surprising number of students in kindergarten to grade 2 also understood that plants need air (78%). This could also be because they know that humans need air and consider plants to need the same things that we do. Many of these students also believed that plants need oxygen (58%) and sometimes explained that they thought that oxygen and air were the same. It was clear, however, that most students at these grade levels were unfamiliar with carbon dioxide and whether plants need it to grow. One student called it "a poison."

In the older grades, students appeared to be more familiar with carbon dioxide. More than half of the students (59%) in grades 3 to 5 and 65 percent of the students in grades 6 to 8 indicated that plants needed it to grow. Sometimes, however, these students indicated that a "reverse" type of breathing was taking place with plants breathing in carbon dioxide and exhaling oxygen. It seems that students learn that oxygen is a product of photosynthesis, but do not understand that the plant also uses oxygen.

Relating the Results to the Standards

The K–4 Standards (NRC 1996) indicate that by the time the students reach fourth grade, they should know that plants need air, water, nutrients, and light. In this study, K–4 students' ideas of plants needing air and water appeared to be unrelated to the production of food. Instead, their explanations included the ideas of the plant needing the air for "breathing" and the water for "drinking."

They also indicated that the Sun provided warmth for the plants, but did not talk about sunlight as necessary for plant growth. These appear to be age-appropriate responses for this group of students.

Only a few kindergarten to grade 2 students identified roots as a common structure of a plant, and some of these students said that potting soil "holds the plant in the ground." It appears that K–2 students need more experiences observing different root systems of plants. Through these observations, they may come to the realization that these structures are an integral part of a plant and that they are not only responsible for anchoring the plant, but also for the transport of water and essential nutrients.

There also appears to be a need to help K–2 students visualize plants as living things. This notion seems to become more prevalent among the views of third to eighth-grade students.

Many of the students in grades 3 to 8 identified air, water, nutrients, and light as important for plant growth. However, students' comments indicated that a good portion of the students in grades 3 to 5 believed that the air was needed for breathing and the water was for plants to drink. It was unclear as to what role the grades 3–5 students believed light and nutrients played in plant growth.

Most middle school students agreed that sunlight and nutrients were important for plant growth; however, their understandings of the components of the grades 5–8 Standards (NRC 1996) dealing with how

Figure 3. Suggestions for Helping Refine Students' Thinking About Plants.

Misconception	Examples of Student Comments	Teaching Idea
Worms help plants grow by getting rid of things that are bad for plants.	"Worms help plants by eating plants and making air holes for plants." "Worms eat bugs that try to eat the plants."	Study real worms in your classroom. By studying worms, students will not only learn about their role as decomposers but will also study other important science standards involving animal characteristics and habitats. (Edwards, Nabors, and Camacho 2002).
Bees do specific things for the purpose of helping plants.	"[Bees] put stuff in the plant to make it grow, like honey." "[The bee] collects moisture, oxygen, honey from one plant and gives it to another."	Organisms carry on activities for the purpose of their own health and survival and, in the process, also become important to other organisms. Do a role-playing pollination simulation with students with a focus on why the bee visits plants and what it does with the nectar it collects.
Soil provides a support structure and food for plants.	"[Soil is] to grow in, and holds it [the plant] so it doesn't wobble." "Plants need soil so they can stand up." "Potting soil is good so plants don't have to grow in dirty soil."	Provide examples of plants that grow in water without soil (e.g., aquariums). Have students germinate seeds in a moist environment, without soil, and in moist soil. They will see that the plant germinates and begins to grow in each case, but does not grow as well without nutrients. They will also see that the stem grows upward and the roots downward.
Sunlight helps plants grow by keeping them warm.	"It warms the plant." [Sunlight] gives plant heat."	Have students grow plants in a warm, lighted environment and compare this with plants grown in a warm, dark environment. Students will see that initially when plants germinate, both sets of plants will grow, but those in the dark are not as green. Over time, the plants in the dark die because, without light, they cannot produce their own food.
Trees and grass are not plants.	"[Grass] but it doesn't make flowers does it?" "No—it's a tree instead of a plant."	Expose students to various plants by visiting a greenhouse or botanical garden. This will help them understand that there are nonflowering plants and plants that do not always have the typical plant parts that students associate with angiosperms.
Plant food is needed for plants to grow.	"Like humans, plants need food to survive." "Everything eats. Plants need food too!"	Engage students in investigations that compare plant growth with and without plant food. In addition, it could be helpful to point out that plant food is actually fertilizer that provides nutrients for plants. It is not a source of food for plants.

plants make food and how energy is passed through an ecosystem were unclear. Plus, the fact that many middle school students still clung to the idea of plants "breathing air" and "drinking water" leads one to believe that they have a limited understanding of how plants make food.

Teaching Implications

In reviewing the results, we found that the students' explanations of what they were thinking—and why—were very helpful in understanding their existing concepts about plants. For example, when a student correctly states that bread mold is not a plant, it is more important to find out why the student has that belief rather than simply focusing on whether the answer is correct. Informal conversations with children can reveal more about their understandings than responses to closed questions.

When responding to whether a telephone pole is a plant, students often used the explanation that the telephone pole is not living and therefore not a plant. They also thought this was a tricky question since it is made from a plant. Similarly, students' responses to pictures of things that can help plants to grow, but may not be absolutely necessary—such as plant food, worms, and bees—often provided us with explanations about how students believe these things help plants to grow.

Even young students appeared to understand many basic characteristics of plants and their needs. Knowing this, teachers can move beyond what is already understood into ideas about plants that students haven't considered. Providing real examples of nonflowering plants or plants without the typical features that students are familiar with

may help them to broaden their understandings. Letting children dig in to observe root structures and consider their functions may help students to think more deeply about how plants are different from animals.

The teacher can also ask questions to highlight ideas that may not be readily observable to students. For example, "What exactly is a bee doing when it travels from flower to flower?" Students' interpretations of this included "delivering things like honey from flower to flower" and "sharing" resources among the flowers. The idea that the bee is obtaining a substance that it needs and, in the process, aiding in plant reproduction is foreign to young students.

Figure 3 on page 138 displays some of the most common student misconceptions about plants revealed in this study. In addition, this table provides suggestions that may help students refine their ideas related to plants and plant growth.

Seek and Share

Like the previous *Science and Children* studies (Barman 1997; Barman et al. 2000), this study provided interesting insights into specific science concepts of students in kindergarten to grade 8. We hope that this study serves as a catalyst to encourage you and your colleagues to seek ways of probing your students' understanding of science concepts and that the findings from this study will help guide your future planning of units dealing with plants.

Charles R. Barman (cbarman@iupui.edu) *is a professor of science and environmental education at Indiana University–Purdue University in Indianapolis, Indiana; Mary Stein*

(stein@oakland.edu) *is an associate professor for the Department of Teacher Development and Educational Studies at Oakland University in Rochester, Michigan; Natalie S. Barman is an instructor of education at Indiana University–Purdue University in Indianapolis, Indiana; and Shannan McNair is an associate professor for the Department of Human Development and Child Studies at Oakland University in Rochester, Michigan.*

Resources

Barker, M. 1995. A plant is an animal standing on its head. *Journal of Biological Education* 29 (3): 203–208.

Barman, C. 1997. Students' views of scientists and science: Results from a national study. *Science and Children* 35 (1): 18–24.

Barman, C., N. Barman, M. L. Cox, K. Newhouse, and M. J. Goldston. 2000. Students' ideas about animals: Results from a national study. *Science and Children* 38 (1): 42–47.

Barman, C., M. Stein, N. Barman, and S. McNair. 2002. Assessing students' ideas about plants. *Science and Children* 10 (1): 25–29.

Bell, B. F. 1981. What is a plant? Some children's ideas. *New Zealand Science Teacher* 31: 10–14.

Edwards, L., M. Nabors, and C. Camacho. 2002. The dirt on worms. *Science and Children* 40 (1): 42–46.

McNair, S., and M. Stein. January 2001. Drawing on their understanding: Using illustrations to invoke deeper thinking about plants. Paper presented at the Association for the Education of Teachers of Science Annual Meeting, Costa Mesa, California.

National Research Council (NRC). 1996. *National Science Education Standards.* Washington, DC: National Academy Press.

Osborne, R. J., and P. Freyberg. 1985. *Learning in science.* London: Heinemann.

Roth, K. 1985. *Food for plants: Teacher's guide.* Research Series No. 153. East Lansing, MI: Michigan State University, Institute for Research on Teaching. (ERIC Document Reproduction Services No. ED # 256 624).

Ryman, D. 1974. Children's understanding of the classification of living organisms. *Journal of Biological Education* 8: 140–144.

Smith, E. L., and C. W. Anderson. 1984. Plants as producers: A case study of elementary science teaching. *Journal of Research in Science Teaching* 21: 685–698.

Stein, M., and S. McNair. January 2002. Science drawings as a tool for analyzing conceptual understanding. Paper presented at the Association for the Education of Teachers of Science Annual Meeting, Charlotte, North Carolina.

Stepens, J. 1985. Biology in elementary schools: Children's conceptions of life. *American Biology Teacher* 47 (4): 222–225.

Tunnicliffe, S. D., and M. J. Reiss. 2000. Building a model of the environment: How do children see plants? *Journal of Biological Education* 34 (4): 172–177.

Acknowledgment

Thank you to the more than 220 teacher-researchers who participated in this study.

Connecting to the Standards

This article relates to the following National Science Education Standards (NRC 1996):

Content Standards

Grades K–4

Standard C: Life Science

- The characteristics of organisms
- Life cycles of organisms
- Organisms and their environments

Grades 5–8

Standard C: Life Science

- Structure and function in living systems
- Reproduction and heredity
- Populations and ecosystems
- Diversity and adaptations of organisms

Let's Try Action Research!

This study reiterated for me the importance of assessing students' background knowledge before planning instruction.

Ginger Stovall and Catherine R. Nesbit

In the late 1990s *Science and Children* extended an invitation to K–8 teachers to participate in a study assessing students' ideas about animals (Barman et al. 1999). More than 180 teachers from across the United States participated. The results, which revealed that many children did not have an understanding of what makes an animal an animal, were reported in a later issue of *Science and Children* (Barman et al. 2000). For example, 80% of K–2 students, 68% of grade 3–5 students, and 50% of grade 6–8 students said a girl was not an animal. The majority of the K–8 students were able to identify the nonhuman mammals—bear, dog, and elephant—as animals while fewer of the students identified invertebrates—jellyfish and octopus—as animals.

When I read the articles in *Science and Children* it piqued my curiosity and prompted me to conduct some action research with my own students. In my study I first determined if my first-grade students had the same misconceptions about animals as the students in Barman et al.'s study. Next, I investigated whether a constructivist approach focusing on students' prior knowledge could alter these misconceptions. This article describes my experiences as I conducted the study and my reflections on the results.

First Assessments

When I began this research, I set out to determine if my first-grade class of 20 students had the same misconceptions as reported by Barman et al. (2000), using the same data collection procedures and materials as in the initial study (Barman et al. 1999).

First, I administered to each student a pretest consisting of an individual interview in which they were asked to sort 18 pictures into two categories, animal and nonanimal. I pulled aside a few students a day while they were engaged in activities at their desks. Because I did not have a large class, I was able to complete this in a few days.

The pictures students sorted included a snail, jellyfish, butterfly, spider, earthworm, octopus, frog, lizard, snake, fish, bird, girl, dog, bear, elephant, mushroom, flower, and oak tree. While the students were sorting the pictures, I tallied their responses. Once the

Figure 1. A Comparison of My First-Grade Students' Perceptions of Animals Versus Students in Barman et al.'s Study (2000).

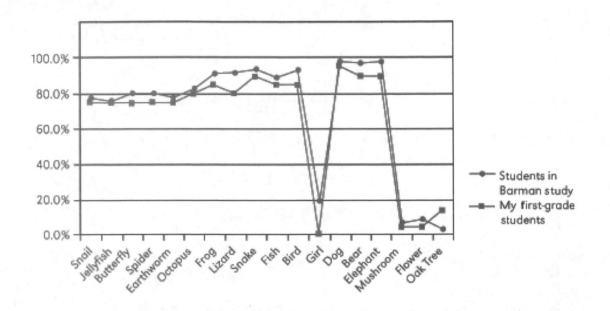

student had sorted all of the pictures I asked, "Why do you think these are animals" and "Why do you think these are not animals?" I then completed the student tally sheets by checking the reason given for each picture. If the child gave a reason that was not listed on the tally sheet, I recorded that response.

When I asked my students why they classified the pictures as they did, many were not sure. Responses I received for why they identified pictures as animals included: "animals have more than two legs," "animals make noises," "animals can fly and swim," "animals are bigger," "they live like animals," and "they look like animals."

Girls Are Animals?

In reviewing the pretest data, I found results similar to those of the Barman study (2000).

A comparison of the two groups' results is shown in Figure 1. The general pattern was the same, although my students were not as accurate.

Many of my students were not able to identify a number of animals. All of the students said that the girl was not an animal. Many students said that the invertebrates—snail, butterfly, spider, octopus, and jellyfish—were not animals. Most of my students looked for four legs, fur, and a tail on the subject to consider it an animal.

Most students were able to identify the mammals—with the exception of the girl—as animals, and the majority of students recognized that plants, mushrooms, and trees were not animals.

As I mentioned earlier, all of my students held the misconception that a girl was not an animal. Many of them even laughed when they saw the picture and questioned why I had put the girl in the stack they were asked to sort.

Other findings revealed students had misconceptions about invertebrates. Five students misidentified a snail, and four students misidentified an octopus and a butterfly as nonanimals.

Again considering the exception of the girl example, fewer students had difficulty identifying vertebrates as animals. Three students misidentified a bird, two students misidentified an elephant and a snake, and one student said a dog was not an animal.

Addressing Misconceptions

Having discovered that many of my first-grade students had misconceptions about animals, I planned to conduct the second part of the study—a one-week constructivist intervention aimed at changing those misconceptions. As recommended in the National Science Education Standards (NRC 1996), I conducted several inquiry lessons with students to address their misconceptions.

Each lesson began with a question that the students could answer by doing an activity. The main question posed was "What does this organism need to survive?" With my help, the students designed a plan to find the answers. They decided to observe organisms and record in their science notebooks what each needed on a daily basis.

Because many students thought invertebrates and people were not animals, I made sure they investigated the needs of invertebrates—spiders and snails—and vertebrates—rabbit, fish, and people.

After several days of observing, students had written answers that included the catego-

ries of air, water, and food. I focused their attention on the food. Specifically, students had written, "spiders ate bugs," "snails ate green scum," "rabbits ate carrots," "fish ate little brown stuff," and "people ate hot dogs."

I guided the students in drawing their own conclusions by asking them many questions, such as "What did the spider need to survive?" (bugs) "What did the person need to survive?" (hot dogs) "How is the spider like a person?" (they both need food). Then I shifted their attention to plants by asking "How are spiders and people different from plants?" (spiders and people need food, and plants do not need food). Based on their observations, I helped them construct scientific meaning from this data using their own words, namely that organisms that need food to survive are called animals and organisms that do not need food are called plants.

Practicing and Reinforcing

Next, the students practiced identifying different plants and animals on nature walks. In addition, they cut out magazine pictures or drew pictures of other animals and plants and identified each one. I made sure they were confronted with pictures of humans during these activities. As part of each of these activities, we discussed whether the organism needed food to survive. If so, the students knew the organism as an animal. If it didn't need food, then it was a plant.

During the intervention, I helped students focus their ideas by talking about what they once thought and what they learned from the inquiry science lessons. I asked them what characteristics they thought something had to have to be considered an

Figure 2. A Comparison of My First-Grade Students' Responses on the Pre- and Posttests.

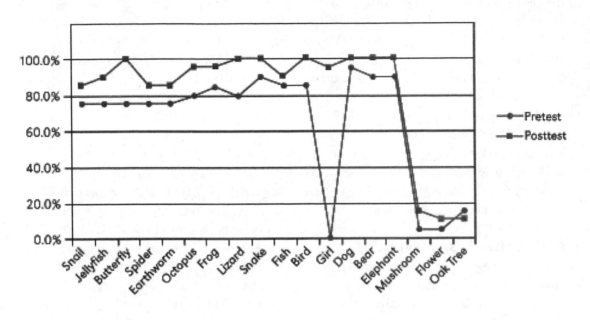

animal. Then I asked them what they used to think an animal was.

We discussed what makes an animal an animal. A typical response I received was that people are animals because they eat food, just like other animals such as dogs. We talked a lot about the fact that humans are classified as animals and why. When we discussed invertebrates, several students said that, even though a snail and a spider did not look like a dog, they were still in the same group called animals because they needed food.

After these inquiry lessons, I reassessed each student to see if his or her perceptions had changed, using the same assessment procedures used at the beginning of the study. I compiled the results and compared them to the pretest to see if a change occurred in their perceptions. I found a marked increase

in their understanding of what an animal is (see Figure 2).

In the posttest, only three students said a snail wasn't an animal and only one student said an octopus was not an animal. Only one student said a girl was not an animal.

Thoughts to Consider

If I were to conduct this study again I would change a few things. First, I would include a comparison group of students holding the same misconceptions as my students who learned the material through a traditional method lacking hands-on activities. By doing this, I could more clearly attribute their changed perceptions about animals to the constructivist approach.

In addition to administering the posttest immediately after the intervention, I would also measure students' perceptions at a later date. By doing this I would see if there were short-term as well as long-term changes in the students' perceptions of animals.

Another thing I would like to do is to conduct the study around our first-grade pet day. I think pet day would be a great opportunity for making new, real-life connections. I would make sure nonmammal pets such as fish, snails, and insects were included on pet day. I would also include a field trip to the zoo.

Last, I would increase the number of participants. Involving all the first-grade students at my school would have allowed us to compare the results in six classrooms.

Teaching and Learning

My results have implications for my future science instruction. This study reiterated for me the importance of assessing students' background knowledge before planning instruction, so that teaching can be planned according to the students' needs and misconceptions.

For example, my students had a good understanding that most mammals were animals. Where I needed to focus my attention was on one particular mammal: the human. I also needed to help them understand that fishes, octopi, butterflies, and snails are also animals.

The second insight I gained from my study was the importance of teaching a concept to students in a developmentally appropriate manner. Many of my students believed that if you were classified as a human or an insect or a fish you couldn't also be classified as an animal. This showed their limited ability to generalize knowledge and categorize objects into subsets. I realized I needed to help my students identify animals

in a concrete way, so I chose the distinguishing characteristic of animals' needing food and plants' not needing food because first-grade students could grasp that concept.

This study also illustrated how difficult it can be to let go of misconceptions. Even after a week of lessons, one student still believed a girl was not an animal. Once a mind has grasped an idea, it can be very difficult to change it. New connections needed to be made by the student in order for previous misconceptions to be altered.

Sometimes, as teachers, we can help students confront a misconception by talking about what they once thought and what they now think. However, if this is unsuccessful, then I often encourage a student who has grasped the concept to talk to the student having difficulty.

Finally, my experience helped me to realize the importance of carefully choosing reading material for students. It is important to remember that, what young children hear or see in books, they believe. For example, if a snake is called a critter in a book they may believe that it is only a critter and cannot be classified as anything else. Teachers must seek out and clarify misleading information for their students.

Can-Do Research

When I first considered conducting this research project, I was reluctant to proceed. However, the *Science and Children* article provided me with the detailed procedure and the materials I needed, so I ventured forth with the project.

Along the way I began to see implications and benefits for my teaching and learning. I believe classroom action research can transform what happens in the classroom. I feel I am a better teacher because of doing this project. Now I can say with confidence that in the future I will continue doing similar investigations with my students.

Ginger Stovall teaches first grade at Welcome Elementary School in Lexington, North Carolina. Catherine R. Nesbit is an associate professor in the Specialty Studies Department at the University of North Carolina at Wilmington.

Resources

Barman, C. R., N. S. Barman, K. Berglund, and M. J. Goldston. 1999. Assessing students' ideas about animals. *Science and Children* 37 (1): 44–49.

Barman, C. R., N. S. Barman, M. L. Cox, K. Newhouse, and M. J. Goldston. 2000. Students' ideas about animals: Results from a national study. *Science and Children* 38 (1): 42–47.

National Research Council (NRC). 1996. *National Science Education Standards.* Washington, DC: National Academy Press.

Connecting to the Standards

This article relates to the following National Science Education Standards (NRC 1996):

Grades K–4

Content Standards

Standard A: Science As Inquiry

- Abilities necessary to do scientific inquiry
- Understanding about scientific inquiry

Standard C: Life Science

Playful Activities for Young Children

Alternative assessments of tasks function well with young children even without any written direction.

Smita Guha and Rodney Doran

As Jennifer watched the water bubbling through the straw, her eyes sparkled. At once, her thoughts flew back to summer days of drinking lemonade and making bubbles with a straw. It was a pleasant, fun-filled memory.

Children relate new experiences to the ones they have already had, scanning every activity through their inquisitive eyes. What can we learn from such an observation? As teachers, we should view experiments through the eyes of young children. We should incorporate familiar objects when designing science experiments to make children's science learning experiences more enjoyable.

As teachers, we need to ask ourselves if the instruction we provide is age appropriate and successful. We also need to incorporate science into daily classroom activities by assessing the science knowledge that a child has and offering appropriate instructional lessons to help him or her become scientifically literate and to generate interest in science.

Alternative assessments in science instruction have been developed for the up-per elementary grades but are limited in the area of early childhood instruction. Because younger children have limited abilities in reading and writing, teachers have difficulty assessing children's scientific knowledge. Early childhood teachers with whom we spoke voiced a need for relevant science assessment for their young students.

We suggest that teachers try the following tasks with children ages four and up, with modifications as needed for age groups. Our intent was to create assessment tasks with appropriate reading and writing demands while at the same time offer activities that use objects familiar to young children. To meet these goals, we used a pictorial format of the tasks that was easy for children to follow and perform.

These activities relate to the National Science Education Standards (NRC 1996) Science as Inquiry Content Standard A (K–4 students should develop abilities necessary to do scientific inquiry and an understanding about scientific inquiry) and Physical Science Content Standard B (K–4 students should develop an understanding of properties

Procedure

We first collected a variety of tasks from books and journals involving science and children (see "Resources"). We examined each task thoroughly and eliminated those that were inappropriate, demanded advanced knowledge in science, or required understanding of specific vocabulary. We selected tasks that fit into two themes: air and water. The tasks selected focused on basic science and involved using easily available, simple materials.

Some tasks described in the books or published in journals did not work and were eliminated. Further, we modified some tasks and supplemented them with materials that were appropriate for young children. We also predicted the answers children would provide as a rationale for each task.

We developed a series of sketches with limited reading material apart from the "Task Title" (see figures 1 through 6). Our intent was to present the sketches to individual four- to six-year-old children who would then perform the tasks step-by-step. Specifically, we told the children to "follow the picture and do the task that the picture shows you to do."

After each task, we asked the children to draw and verbally describe what they observed. Some children could write down answers, and some could not. We taped the answers of those who could not write. After each task performance, we asked the children to describe what they did and why they thought it happened. We evaluated the individual performance of the tasks with a small

group of children, then revised the tasks that needed modification and administered those tasks to a large group of students on an individual basis.

The first task served as a warm-up activity. We helped students perform this initial activity so they would become familiar with performing tasks using picture directions.

Figure 1. Paper Spinner.

Paper Spinner

For this activity, we wanted to find out if children could identify that air causes paper to spin. We cut the paper and asked the child to hold the paper and fold one part one way and the other part the other way (see Figure 1). Then students slid a paper clip onto the paper. Finally, we asked the child to climb up some stairs and release the paper. The child observed as the paper spun toward the ground.

Next, we asked the child to do the experiment with no paper clip and then with more than one paper clip. The child observed that with no paper clip the paper did not spin at all, and with more paper clips the paper spun a number of times. However, if there were more than seven clips, the student noticed that the paper did not spin at all. We asked the child to observe the number of rotations when the paper was dropped from different heights. Some children were verbal enough to tell us that "as the paper goes down, it spins" or "the paper is going round and round."

We were assessing "Does air move paper?" However, none of the children could relate the task with air.

Fly Away

Fly Away was an activity in which the children crumpled up a piece of tissue paper and placed it in the mouth of a transparent soda bottle (see Figure 2). Students tried blowing the paper into the bottle. We wanted to find out if children could identify that the air inside the bottle does not allow the paper to go inside. This is a discrepant event because the children predicted that on blowing, the paper would go inside the bottle, but in reality, the paper flew out of the bottle.

We wanted to assess "Does air block the mouth of the bottle? (Does air occupy space?)" Only 2 out of 16 children answered that it was the air in the bottle that stopped the paper from going inside.

Blowing Into Water

Students performed this next task by blowing up a balloon, putting the mouth of the balloon on one end of a straw, and placing the other end of the straw into a jar of water (see Figure 3). For hygienic purposes, we gave a new straw and a new balloon to each child. We wanted to see if children could identify that air causes water to bubble.

Figure 3. Blowing Into Water.

Most of the children could not blow up the balloon by themselves. In those cases, we either blew up the balloon for them or made the task self-sufficient, having children blow directly through the straw. As the air left the balloon and went through the straw into the water, the children noticed bubbles coming out of the straw.

We wanted to assess "Does the air make the water bubble?" Some of the typical responses were "The bubbles formed in water because of air," "We have lots of air in our mouth," and "The air comes from my mouth, through the straw, goes into the water, and makes bubbles."

Although air is all around us, we seldom think about it until we visualize it. However,

Figure 2. Fly Away.

children could relate some of these activities to events in their daily lives. For example, by blowing through a straw into a jar full of water, a child was reminded of her grandmother's pool where she observed bubbles coming out through a filter.

A similar task was blowing into a pan of water. The children blew through a straw onto a pan of water. The typical response was "Water is moving away," indicating waves in the water. Some children even drew the picture of waves in water. When we asked "Why did they think water was moving away?" the common answer was "Because I am blowing."

"What are you blowing?" we asked. "Air" was the typical response.

Mover

For this task, we wanted to find out if children could identify that air is what causes paper dots in water to move. Children dropped colored paper dots into a pan of water. When they blew air into the pan of water, the dots made a whirling motion in the water (see Figure 4). The children were excited and said, "The dots are moving out of my way" and "The dots are going round and round."

We wanted to assess "Does air move the dots in the water?" We asked, "Why do you think the dots are moving?" The most common answer was "Because I am blowing them away."

In the previous three activities (blowing into water, blowing into a pan of water, and mover), most of the children were able to relate the tasks with the concept of air.

Figure 4. Mover.

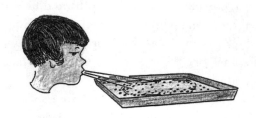

Float or Sink

In the next task, the children predicted whether object such as corks, bottle tops, pebbles, and soap would float or sink. We wanted to find out if children could understand that shape or size does not cause objects to float or sink. They then performed the float or sink activity to determine if their prediction was correct. In this task, we asked questions using words we thought each child could understand. For example, in some cases, we used *sit down* or *stay down* instead of the word *sink* because some children had a hard time understanding the term *sink*.

We wanted to assess "Does shape or size not help objects to float or sink?" The children confidently predicted which objects sank and which floated. Following this task, we asked the children if they could say why some objects floated and some sank. Some children said, "because of different shape" and "because some of them are big and some small," while others said, "Some are heavy and some are light."

Cup and Water

Cup and water was another discrepant event that amazed the children. We wanted to see if children could identify that air inside the cup does not let the water go inside the cup.

Figure 5. Cup and Water.

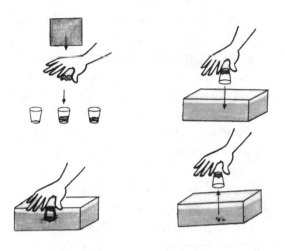

In this activity, we stuck a piece of tissue paper inside a transparent cup with adhesive tape (see Figure 5). We asked the children, "What do you think will happen if you put anything in water?" They all said, "It will get wet." Then we asked the children, "What will happen to the tissue in the cup if you put the cup upside down in the water?" Most of the children predicted that the tissue in the cup would get wet if the cup was put under water.

We wanted to assess "Does air block water to move up the cup. (Does air occupy space?)" Some children identified that air in the cup would not let the tissue get wet. Most of the children tried to investigate the cause by pouring more water in the transparent box, so that the whole cup went under water.

Bottle Organ

This activity involved pouring water at various levels into different glass bottles. By striking the bottles with a spoon, different-sounding notes are made (see Figure 6). We

wanted to see if children could understand that different sounds are produced when there is a different amount of water in each bottle (i.e., a different amount of air). It was quite exciting to the children. They were delighted to hear the sounds and exclaimed, "Bottles are making music!"

Figure 6. Bottle Organ.

We were assessing "Does the amount of water cause different sound?" Most of the children could identify the highest and lowest sound and that the sound change from one bottle to another was because of the different water levels. Few children, however, identified air above the water level in the bottles as being involved with the sounds.

Playful Assessment

Children responded to these tasks in different ways. They predicted the results before performing each activity and then interpreted their observations verbally and through sketches. We observed the children's actions and noted that, while performing the tasks, the four-year-old children appeared to discover phenomena about the tasks, while most of the five-year-old children could identify the cause of the happenings.

For example, some four-year-old students could not answer what was inside the inflated balloon that made it big in the blowing-into-water task. When we deflated the balloon on their hands so they could feel the air coming out, the four-year-old students discovered in amazement that it was air inside the balloon that made it become big, whereas most of the five-year-old students knew that the air made it big and made bubbles in the water.

These activities were not only enjoyable to the children but also provided teachers with some knowledge about alternative assessment in early childhood education. After presenting the tasks at workshops, teachers tried them in their classrooms and enjoyed watching children perform the activities. These hands-on experiments provided evidence that such projects can be incorporated into classroom teaching.

One teacher remarked, "The science experiments were interesting and practical. It was good to learn how science can be applied to early childhood education. Most of the time, we tend to shy away from science, especially in early childhood education." Another teacher commented that children loved paper spinner and float or sink ". . . since young children enjoy watching objects move." According to another teacher, "these pictures with activities are also an excellent idea for children with limited language proficiency or with minimal reading or writing ability."

From the activities that the children performed and the teachers' responses, the following could be learned:

- Children can be assessed using activities in a playful setting.
- Alternative assessments of tasks function well with young children even without any written direction.
- Children can provide reasonable insight to the teachers, and teachers in turn can learn from children's activities about the level of performance as they design and construct their lesson plans in science teaching.
- Hands-on activities provide better understanding of the concept, and, if done through playful activities, learning is more relevant and enjoyable.

Smita Guha is an assistant professor in the college of education at Temple University in Philadelphia, Pennsylvania, and Rodney Doran is a professor at State University of New York at Buffalo.

Resources

National Research Council (NRC). 1996. *National Science Education Standards*. Washington, DC: National Academy Press.

Strongin, H. 1991. *Science on a shoestring*. 2nd ed. Reading, MA: Addison-Wesley Longman.

Tolman, M. N., and J. O. Morton. 1986. *Earth science activities for grades 2–8*. Book III. New York: Parker Publishing.

VanCleave, J. 1991. *Earth science for every kid*. New York: John Wiley & Sons.

VanCleave, J. 1991. *Physics for every kid*. New York: John Wiley & Sons.

Also in Science and Children

Barrow, L., R. Litherland, S. Bajpai, J. Smith, and J. Parker. 1997. Super bubble and for fingers only. *Science and Children* 34 (6): 46–48.

Colburn, K., and P. Tate. 1998. The big yellow laboratory. *Science and Children* 36 (1): 22–25.

Connecting to the Standards

This article relates to the following National Science Education Standards (NRC 1996):

Grades K–4

Content Standards

Standard A: Science As Inquiry

- Abilities necessary to do scientific inquiry
- Understanding about scientific inquiry

Grades K–4

Standard B: Physical Science Content

- Students should develop an understanding of properties of objects and materials and position and motion of objects.

Index

ability levels, and science learning centers 54

access, and science learning centers 54

activities, for young children 151–57

Adams, D. 21

advertisement, of Science Night of Fun 66

age

    early childhood and interest in science 3–4

    and early learning of science by very young children vii–viii

    and Playful Activities for Young Children 155–56

    See also grade levels; preschool children

air

    and growth requirements of plants 139

    and Playful Activities for Young Children 153–54, 155

Alaska, and The Bird project 29–31

alternative assessments, and Playful Activities for Young Children 151–57

animals

    background knowledge and identification of 146–47, 148

    integrating drawing with learning about 122–23

    relatives sizes of 22–23

    See also zoo; zoology

applied learning projects 57, 59

Arizona State University West 53

art

    and connection with science 121

    and Ladybugs Across the Curriculum, 100

    and Students' Ideas About Plants 135–43

    and Tree of Life 132

    See also collage; drawing; painting

Arthropoda 39
assessment
      and Drawing on Student Understanding 121–27
      goals and examples of x–xi
      and Let's Try Action Research! 145–50
      and Playful Activities for Young Children 151–57
      of students' work with relative sizes 24–25
      and Tree of Life 129–34
Avila, Carol viii

background knowledge, assessing of students' before planning instruction
      145–50
bacteria, and safety 46, 47
ballooning, by spiders 40
Barman, Charles R. xi, 146
Barman, Natalie S. xi
Beckett, Carol ix
bees, and plants 140
benefits
      of birdwatching program 77
      of classroom science centers 55–56
Biggest, Strongest, Fastest (Jenkins 1995) 22
Bird, The, and child-centered curricula 29–31
birds
      and bird watching program 73–78
      and project based on found object 29–31
black widow spider 41
blocks, and Science and Mathematics of Building Structures 85–91
blowing into water activity 153–54
blueprints, for Miniature Sleds 107, 108
bodily-kinesthetic intelligence 98, 100–101
books
      Ladybugs Across the Curriculum and class-published 99
      and Tree of Life program 129–34
      See also literature; resources
botany, and early childhood career learning centers 5
      See also plants
bottle organ activity 155
box turtles 58
brochure, for reptile exhibit 62
Brown, Skila King xi
brown recluse spider 41
Bugs (Parker & Wright 1987) 124

bulbs and bulbets, and tulips 83
Butcher, Jan x, 122
butterflies 131

carbon dioxide 139
cardinals 74, 76
careers, and interest of young children in science 4, 5
carnivores 42
Castellitto, Andrea ix
celebration, and testing of Miniature Sleds designs 109–10
centripetal force 35
cephalothorax, of spider 39
Chalufour, Ingrid ix–x
Charlotte's Web (White 1974) 41
chickadee 76
child-centered curricula
     The Bird 29–31
     It's a Frog's Life 45–51
     Project Reptile 57–64
     Reggio Emilia approach 33–37
     and science learning centers 53–56
     Science Night of Fun, 65–70
     Spiderrific Learning Tools 39–44
classification, of items as plants or not plants 136–37
class projects, and Project Reptile 57–64
classroom
     and bird feeding station 73–74
     and construction center for Miniature Sleds 106–107
     and cultivating early interest in science 4
     and early science instruction for very young children xi
     and science learning centers 53–56
     and Science and Mathematics of Building Structures 86–87
     See also discussions
cobweb 40, 41
Coffey, Audrey ix
collaborative school culture 113–14
collage, and sense of touch 116
communication, and Kids Questioning Kids: "Experts" Sharing 7–8
     See also discussions; language skills; listening; questions and
        questioning
community
     and collaborative partnership with classroom 117
     as resource for classroom science instruction 18–19

computers
        See e-mail; Journey North educational program; SciLinks
construction center, for Miniature Sleds 105
constructivist intervention, and student misconceptions 147
cornea, of eye 114, 116
county agricultural extension agents 80–81
crab spiders 40–41
cultural objects, and science centers 54
        See also collaborative school culture; difference; diversity
cup and water activity 154–55
curriculum
        See child-centered curricula; integrating curricula

dance, and Ladybugs Across the Curriculum 100–101
data collection, and Students' Ideas About Plants 136
Davis, Dorothy ix
death
        and The Bird project 30, 31
        and It's a Frog's Life 51
Design Technology: Children's Engineering (Dunn & Larson 1990) 105
DeSouza, Josephine Shireen viii–ix
developmental spelling 58, 61
Dias, Michael x
Diem, Keith ix
difference, science learning centers and celebration of students' 53–54
Diffily, Deborah ix
directions, for science learning centers 55
Discovery Central xiii, 93–95
discussions, in classroom
        communication skills and 7–8
        documentation of 7
        and Ladybugs Across the Curriculum 99
        of shadows 10–12
dissection, of cow's eye 117
diversity, in classrooms and science learning centers 53, 55
docents, for reptile exhibit 62
doctors, and visits to classroom 115–16
Doran, Rodney ix
do, reflect, and apply, and 4-H science programs 41
drawing
        and Drawing on Student Understanding project 121–27
        and relative sizes of animals and insects 22–23
Duckworth, Eleanor 16

ear, and hearing 115
early learning and science
        How Big is Big?: How Small is Small? 21–25
        Kids Questioning Kids: "Experts" Sharing 7–13
        Start Young! 3–6
        What the Real Experts Say 15–19
Earth science, and early childhood career learning centers 5
        See also geology
eggs, of frogs 45, 47–49
e-mail, and research on reptiles 58–59
engineering, and Miniature Sleds project 105–11
English language, and science learning centers 54, 55
entomologists 44, 101
environment
        Reggio Emilia approach and structuring of 33–34
        and Tree of Life program 129–34
        See also habitat
equinoxes 9
evaluations, of students' work with relative sizes 24–25
        See also assessment
Exhibits
        and Project Reptile 59–62
        and Tree of Life 131
        See also open house
experience, and exposure to science at early ages vii, viii
        See also observation
Experts
        See doctors; nurses; scientists
Exploration
        See open exploration; outdoor exploration
Extension Service, of Department of Agriculture 41, 80–81
eye and eyesight, and senses 114, 116, 117

facilitators, for discussions 10, 12
fact cards 58, 59
Family Math program 65
Farmer's Almanac calendar 82
feeling boxes 116–17
field trips
        and It's a Frog's Life 49
        and Journey Into the Five Senses 117
        and Let's Try Action Research! 149
        and Project Reptile 58

See also nature walks; science museums; zoo

fifth grade, and Science Night of Fun 67

See also grade levels

First Flight program 73–79

first grade

and Let's Try Action Research! 145–50

and Science Night of Fun 67

and Tracking Through the Tulips 79–84

and What the Real Experts Say 15–19

See also grade levels

flight path, of birds 75–76

float or sink activity 154

fly away activity 153

follow-up experiences, and program on spiders 43–44

food, and characteristics of plants 135–36, 138, 140, 141.

See also nutrition

food chain 31

force, Reggio Emilia approach and study of 34, 35, 36

forest ranger, and visit to classroom 30–31

4-H science programs 39, 41

14 forest Mice and the Winter Sledding Day, The (Iwamura 1991) 105

fourth grade, and Science Night of Fun 67

See also grade levels

friction 35, 36

funnel web 40

Gardner, Howard 98, 102

geology, and science centers 54

See also Earth science

giraffes 21, 22, 25

gnomon 9

Goodall Jane 3

grade levels, and identification of plants 136–37.

See also fifth grade; first grade; fourth grade; kindergarten; preschool children; second grade; third grade

grass, and identification of plants 137, 140

gravity and gravitational pull 35, 36

Grouchy Ladybug, The (Carle 1986) 98, 101

group work, and science learning centers 54

growth, plant requirements for 137–39

Guha, Smita xi

habitat, of frogs, 50

See also environment

Hamm, M. 21

Head Start program 85

hearing, sense of 115

height, of structures built with blocks 88–89

Herb Kohl Educational Foundation 107

hobbies, and early interest of children in science 4

Hoisington, Cindy ix–x

Horner, Jack 3

house finch 74, 76

How Big is Big? How Small is Small? viii, 21–25

humans

      identification of as animals 146–47, 148, 149

      attribution of characteristics of to plants 135–36, 138

hummingbirds 73, 74, 76–77

inertia 35, 36

inquiry-based learning strategies

      and National Science Education Standards 7

      and project on five senses 113–18

insects

      drawing and learning about 121, 122, 124, 126

      and Ladybugs Across the Curriculum 99

      relative sizes of, 22–23; and safety 123

      and spiders 39–41

integrating curricula

      Discovery Central 93–95

      First Flight 73–78

      Journey Into the Five Senses 113–18

      Ladybugs Across the Curriculum 97–103

      Miniature Sleds 105–11

      Science and Mathematics of Building Structures 85–91

      Tracking Through the Tulips 79–84

interdisciplinary teaching strategies 133

interpersonal and intrapersonal intelligence 98, 101–102

invertebrates, and identification of animals 146

invitations, to reptile exhibit 62

Irwin, Leslie ix

It's a Frog's Life xii 45–51

Iwasyk, Marletta viii

Jereb, Jill viii–ix

journal, and Ladybugs Across the Curriculum 98

Journey Into the Five Senses xiii, 113–18
Journey North educational program 79–84

Keller, Helen 113
Kids Questioning Kids: "Experts" Sharing 7–13
kid-watching skills 108–109
kindergarten
    and Discovery Central 93–95
    and First Flight 73–78
    and Ladybugs Across the Curriculum 97–103
    and Miniature Sleds 105–11
    and Project Reptile 57–64
    and Science Night of Fun 67
    and Tracking Through the Tulips 79–84
kitchen chemistry 5
KWHL charts 10, 94

Ladybugs Across the Curriculum xiii, 97–103
language skills
    and Ladybugs Across the Curriculum 98–99
    Miniature Sleds and engineering terminology 109
    and vocabulary of building structures 87–88
    See also communication; English language; writing
Learning
    and student-centered approach to science viii–ix
    Tree of Life and preparation for further 131, 133
    See also early learning and science; inquiry-based learning
        strategies; science learning centers
learning centers
    See science learning centers
Lego's blocks 87
Let's Try Action Research! xiii, 145–50
letters, and Project Reptile 58
levers
    and Miniature Sleds 109
    and Reggio Emilia approach 34
life cycle
    of birds 31
    of frogs 49, 50, 51
    of ladybugs 100
    See also death; eggs; food chain
Lifetimes (Rice 1997) 23
linguistic intelligence 98–99

National Science Teachers Association

listening
    and classroom discussions 8
    and sense of hearing 115
Listening Walk, The (Showers 1991) 115
literature, relative sizes and integrating of 22–23, 25.
        See also books; journal
Living Bird (Cornell Lab) 76
logical-mathematical intelligence 98, 99
Lowry Center for Early Childhood Education (Michigan) 121, 122, 123, 124

machines, and Reggio Emilia approach 33–37
MacShara, Jeannie xi
mammals, and identification of animals 146, 149
materials, diversity in for science learning centers 55
mathematics
    and Ladybugs Across the Curriculum 99
    quantification of data and integrating of science and 21
    and Science and Mathematics of Building Structures 85–91
    and Tree of Life 132
McNair, Shannan x, 135
McWilliams, Susan x
Measurement
    and How Big is Big? How Small is Small? 21–25
    of tulips grown from bulbs 15–16
microscope, and study of pond water 50
Miniature Sleds, Go, Go, Go! xiii, 105–11
Misconceptions
    and assessing student's background knowledge 145–50
    of students about plants 140, 141
Missouri Department of Education 93
Mitchell, Kevin ix
models and modeling
    design of wheels and use of 18
    of eye 116
    and relative sizes of animals 22
    teachers as 126
mold, and plants 136, 141
molting, of insects 101
Moriarty, Robin ix–x
mosquito larvae, and ponds 46, 47
motion
    Reggio Emilia approach and study of 34
    wheels and study of 17–18

mover activity 154
multiple intelligences 97–103
museums
      See science museums
mushrooms 136, 137
music and musical intelligence
      and bottle organ activity 155
      and Ladybugs Across the Curriculum 98, 101

National Council of Teachers of Mathematics Principles and Standards for
      School Mathematics (NCTM 2000) 86, 89
National Science Education Teaching Standards (NSES)
      criteria for teaching of science vii
      Discovery Central xiii, 95
      Drawing on Student Understanding xiii, 121
      How Big is Big? How Small is Small? viii, xii, 21
      and inquiry-based learning strategies 7
      It's a Frog's Life xii, 50
      Journey Into the Five Senses xiii, 118
      Kids Questioning Kids: "Experts" Sharing 8
      Ladybugs Across the Curriculum xiii, 103
      Let's Try Action Research xiii, 150
      Miniature Sleds xiii, 111
      Playful Activities for Young Children xiii, 151, 157
      Project Reptile xii, 57, 63
      quick-reference chart for xii–xiii
      Reggio Emilia approach xii, 35–37
      Science Centers for All xiii
      Science and Mathematics of Building Structures xiii, 86, 91
      Science Night of Fun xii, 70
      Spiderrific Learning Tools xii, 44
      Students' Ideas About Plants xiii, 135, 136, 143
      Tracking Through the Tulips xiii, 84
      Tree of Life xiii, 134
      What the Real Experts Say 15, 19
National Science Teachers Association (NSTA), and safety guidelines 46,
      123
naturalist intelligence 98, 102
nature walks
      and bird watching 74–76
      and identifying different plants and animals 147
      and Ladybugs Across the Curriculum 102
Nesbit, Catherine R. xi

New Jersey 4-H Science Discovery Series 39, 41
Newton, Isaac 17
Nicci, Christine ix
Nice, Margaret Morse 74–76
nose, and sense of smell 115
nurses, and visits to classroom 30
nutrition, and early childhood career learning centers 5
   See also food; food chain

observation, and Journey Into the Five Senses 114
oceanography, and early childhood career learning centers 5
open exploration, and Science and Mathematics of Building Structures
   87–88
open house, and Science and Mathematics of Building Structures 89
orb webs 40, 41
ornithologist 76
outdoor exploration, and Ladybugs Across the Curriculum 102
oxygen, and plants 139

painting, with objects from nature 94
paleontology, and early childhood career learning centers 5
paper chromatography 17
paper spinner activity 152–53
parents and parental involvement
   and Miniature Sleds 106, 107
   and Reggio Emilia approach 36–37
   and Science Night of Fun 66, 68, 69
pet day 149
photograph display, and reptile exhibit 61
photosynthesis 139
planning, of Science Night of Fun 65–66
plants
   Discovery Central and science learning centers 93–95
   growing tulips from bulbs and measurement of 15–16
   and Students' Ideas About Plants 135–43
   and Tracking Through the Tulips program 79–84
   See also botany
Playful Activities for Young Children xiii, 151–57
Plummer, Donna M. xi
pond water, and It's a Frog's Life 46, 47, 49–50
positive reinforcement, and Science Night of Fun 68–69
posttest, and identification of plants and animals 148
practicing, of identification of plants and animals 147–48

predators 42
preschool children
        and It's a Frog's Life, 45–51
        and Science and Mathematics of Building Structures 85–91
preservice teachers, and Science Night of Fun 65–66, 68–69
Primarily Plants (Hoover and Mercier 1990) 93
Project Reptile xii, 57–64
pulleys, and Miniature Sleds project 109

questions and questioning
        and building structures with blocks 88–89
        and development of communication skills for modeling 8, 12
        and program on frogs and tadpoles 48

rain forest
        animals of 124–25
        and Tree of Life program 129–34
Rain Forest (Cowcher 1990) 131
rat snakes 58
reading, and thematic web for Tree of Life 132
reflection, and Ladybugs Across the Curriculum 101–102
        See also do, reflect, and apply
Reggio Emilia approach xiii, 33–37
reinforcing, and identification of plants and animals 147–48
        See also positive reinforcement
reptiles, and Project Reptile 57–64
research
        and learning about reptiles 58–59
        and Let's Try Action Research! 145–50
resources
        and bibliography for Ladybugs Across the Curriculum 100
        community, a 18–19
        for Drawing on Student Understanding 126
        trade books and Tree of Life 133
        See also SciLinks
Rommel-Esham, Katie ix
roots, of plants 139
Rubin, Penni viii

Safety
        and handling of dead bird 29
        and spiders 41
        and tools 107–108

and wading pools or ponds 46, 47

    with insects and animals 123

Sammy's Science House CD-ROM (Edmark 1996) 108

sapsuckers 77

Sarow, Gina x

Scheduling

    for Reptiles Exhibit Project 57

    of time for science learning centers 54

science

    connecting drawings with 121, 124

    and early learning by very young children vii–viii

    and student-centered approach to learning viii–ix

    and thematic web for Tree of Life 132

    See also early learning and science; science learning centers;
        scientists

Science and Children 25, 46, 135, 141, 145, 149

Science Centers for All xii, 53–56

science learning centers

    career-oriented for early childhood 5

    and Discovery Central program 93–95

    and Ladybugs Across the Curriculum 99

    and Science Centers for All program 53–56

Science and Mathematics of Building Structures xiii, 85–91

science museums

    and Journey Into the Five Senses 117

    and Project Reptile 58, 61

Science Night of Fun xii, 65–70

Scientists

    and interviews about early interest in science 3

    inviting to classroom 4, 44, 101, 124–25

    and studies of historic figures 17, 74–76

    See also doctors; nurses

SciLinks

    and birds 75

    and insects 122

    and reptiles 58

    an senses 114

    and simple machines 34

second grade

    and How Big is Big? How Small is Small? 21–25

    and Science Night of Fun 67

    and Tracking Through the Tulips 79–84

    See also grade levels

seeds: and Discovery Central program 94, 95
        and Students' Ideas About Plants 137
senses, and Journey Into the Five Senses 113–18
shadows, and activity suggestions 9, 10–12
sheet web 40
show-and-tell time 8
simplicity, in directions for science centers 55
size, and How Big is Big? How Small is Small? viii, 21–25
        See also measurement
smell, sense of 115
social skills, and Ladybugs Across the Curriculum 101
soil, and plants 81, 140
solstices 9
songs, and Ladybugs Across the Curriculum 101
Spiderrific Learning Tools xii, 39–44
spiders, and Spiderrific Learning Tools 39–44
spider webs 40, 41, 42–43
spinnerets, of spiders 39, 40
spiracles, of insects 22
Start Young! 3–6
State University of New York College at Genesco 65
Stein, Mary x, xi, 135
Sterling, Donna ix
Still More Activities that Teach (Jackson 2000) 110
Stokes Beginner's Guide to Birds (Stokes and Stokes 1996) 73, 74
Stovall Ginger, xi
Students' Ideas About Plants xiii
STUFF (Stimulating Tools Useful for Fun and Fundamentals) 4, 5
Successlink (Missouri Department of Education) 93
sunplot/shadow board 9
sun and sunlight
        activity suggestions for plots and shadows 9
        and growth requirements of plants 138–39, 140
        and Tracking Through the Tulips 82–83

tadpoles 45, 47, 48–49
take home activities, and Science Night of Fun 67, 68
tape recorders
        and directions for science centers 55
        and documenting classroom discussions 7
tarantulas 39–40
taste, and senses 115–16
teachable moments 45

teachers and teaching
>implications of student misconceptions about plants and animals for 141, 149
>and professional development workshop 80
>as role models 126
>*See also* classroom; learning; preservice teachers

Tennessee Science Teachers Association 79

terrariums, and frogs 50, 51

testing, of Miniature Sleds designs 109–10
>*See also* assessment; evaluation; posttest

thematic web, and Tree of Life 129–30, 132, 133

think-pair-share strategies 101

third grade, and Science Night of Fun 67

thorax, of insect 124

Tigger's Contraptions CD-ROM (Disney 1997) 108

Time
>*See* scheduling; timeline

timeline, for reptiles exhibit project 60

titmice 76

tongue, and sense of taste 115–16

tools, and Miniature Sleds project 107–108

touch, sense of 116–17

towers, and building structures with blocks 88–89

Toyota Tapestry Grant 79, 80

Tracking Through the Tulips xiii, 79–84

tree(s)
>and identification of plants 136, 137, 140
>and The Tree of Life program 129–34

Tree of Life, The xiii 129–34

Tree of Life: The World of the African Baobab (Bash 1989) 129–34

trial and error, and building structures with blocks 87

tulips 15–16, 79–84

U.S. Department of Agriculture 41

U.S. Geological Survey 3

Universities
>and bird watching program, 74
>and Science Night program 65–70

University of Alaska–Southeast 29

University of Colorado at Denver 113

University of Washington 8

Upland Hills School (Michigan) 121, 123

Venn diagram 86, 89–90

verbal-linguistic intelligence 98

video cameras, and documenting classroom discussions 7

vision

    See eye and eyesight

visual-spatial intelligence 98, 99–100

Vygotsky L. S. 16

Ward, Christina Dias x

Warren on Wheels Festival 18–19

water, and plant growth 139

    See also pond water

West Nile virus 47

What the Real Experts Say 15–19

What's Smaller Than a Pygmy Shrew (Wells 1995) 23

wheels, and study of motion 17–18

Whitin, Phyllis ix

Winokur, Jeff ix–x

Wisconsin, and Miniature Sleds project 105

wondering, science as 8

Wood, Jaimee x

woodpeckers 77

worms 140

Worth, Karen ix–x

writing, and thematic web for Tree of Life 132

    See also books; developmental spelling; journal; letters; literature

zone of proximal development 16, 17

zoo, and field trips 58, 149

zoology

    and early childhood career learning centers 5

    rain forest animals and visit to classroom by zoologist 124–25